DESTROYER
CAPTAIN

DESTROYER CAPTAIN

THE LIFE OF ERNEST E. EVANS

**James D. Hornfischer and
David J. Hornfischer**

CALIBER

DUTTON CALIBER
An imprint of Penguin Random House LLC
penguinrandomhouse.com

LIBRARY OF CONGRESS CATALOGING-IN-PUBLICATION DATA

Names: Hornfischer, James D., author. | Hornfischer, David J., author.
Title: Destroyer captain : the life of Ernest E. Evans / James D.
Hornfischer, and David J. Hornfischer. Other titles: Life of Ernest E. Evans
Description: New York : Dutton Caliber, [2024]
Identifiers: LCCN 2023050355 (print) | LCCN 2023050356 (ebook) |
ISBN 9780593184677 (trade paperback) | ISBN 9780593184684 (ebook)
Subjects: LCSH: Evans, Ernest Edwin, 1908–1944. | United States.
Navy—Officers—Biography. | Leyte Gulf, Battle of, Philippines, 1944. |
World War, 1939–1945—Naval operations, American. | Johnston
(Destroyer : DD 557) | World War, 1939–1945—Participation, Indian.
Classification: LCC D774.L48 E934 2024 (print) | LCC D774.L48 (ebook) |
DDC 940.54/2599092 [B]—dc23/eng/20240301
LC record available at https://lccn.loc.gov/2023050355
LC ebook record available at https://lccn.loc.gov/2023050356

Printed in the United States of America
1st Printing

BOOK DESIGN BY ALISON CNOCKAERT

To all the writers and military historians who
keep these stories of heroism
and valor alive and in our collective
consciousness

This is going to be a fighting ship. I intend to go in harm's way, and anyone who doesn't want to go along had better get off right now.

COMMANDER ERNEST E. EVANS
TAKING COMMAND OF USS JOHNSTON (DD-557),
OCTOBER 27, 1943

Table of Contents

CONTENTS

Author's Note

I am very proud that *Destroyer Captain: The Life of Ernest E. Evans* has been chosen as the final chapter of the American War Hero Series. This author note will offer the reader an opportunity to explore and dive deeper into Captain Evans's life as well as the life of his crew and the fate of the USS *Johnston*.

Captain Ernest E. Evans is a very fitting member to this esteemed list of fighter pilots, medal of honor recipients, paratroopers, marine legends and historic World War II battles that have been highlighted in the American War Hero book series.

My father, James D. Hornfischer, and I were honored to be tasked to coauthor a memoir of Captain Evans's heroic life of service for this series. This book is to be an extensive look into this trailblazer of a man's service to our country, and an intimate look into the character, ambition, and heroism of Captain Evans from his early life in Oklahoma, to his Naval Academy days, to World War II. Captain Evans's leadership was apparent early in his life, and he became one of the first Native Americans to attend and graduate from the U.S. Naval Academy, class of 1931.

Captain Evans of the USS *Johnston* lost his life in the Battle of Leyte Gulf on October 25, 1944. This David and Goliath story is immortalized in my father's book *The Last Stand of the Tin Can Sailors* (Bantam, 2004) and expanded upon in his 2004 C-SPAN interview.

In 2021, exploration crews identified and surveyed the wreck of USS *Johnston*, which was discovered seventy-seven years after its sinking at the Battle of Leyte Gulf.

In fall 2023, Secretary of the Navy Carlos Del Toro honored Evans by naming an Arleigh *Burke*-class ship USS *Ernest E. Evans*.

These stories are more than mere facts about bygone days; they are stories of heroism, leadership character, and work ethic. It is my hope that future generations can learn from studying the bravery, service and sacrifice of Captain Evans and his crew and keep these stories alive to inspire patriotism that will continue to keep American ingenuity and leadership at the forefront of the world.

DESTROYER CAPTAIN

CHAPTER 1

The Nail That Stands Up Gets Hammered Down

AUGUST 1908–JUNE 1931

Oklahoma in 1908, the year after winning its statehood, was deeply imprinted with the United States' long history of bad faith toward Native Americans and of the seizing of their land first by conquest, then by broken treaty, and finally by fraud. In many ways, Oklahoma was the summation of it. During the frontier era, no fewer than forty native nations were driven off their ancestral lands and forced to accept small reservations on this rectangle in the middle of the country. Then in 1883 and the following years, even those tribal lands were taken from them; individual families were given small allotments, and the remainder was opened to white settlement. In 1890 the territory was named "Oklahoma," Choctaw for "the land of red men."

Eastern Oklahoma was dominated by five nations from the American Southeast who were the first to be compelled to surrender their lands to Anglo-Americans: the Cherokee, Chickasaw, Choctaw, Creek, and Seminole. Because of their partial adoption

1

of American culture, they became known collectively as the "Five Civilized Tribes."

Once in Oklahoma, it was the Cherokee in the northeast who claimed a kind of preeminence. Partly this was because a native genius, Sequoyah, had given them an alphabet and written language generations before, so they were almost fully literate, and partly it was because they had tried harder than any other nation to placate white Americans by adopting an American way of life. In their native lands in Georgia, they had owned slaves and plantations. It had done them no good, and they had been sent west, most in the horrifying "Trail of Tears." Seventy miles southwest of the Cherokee capital of Tahlequah lay the Creek capital of Okmulgee. Of the five tribes, the Creek were perhaps the fiercest warriors. When they had lived on their lands in Alabama, their opposition to American rule had reached its high point when they allied themselves with the British in the War of 1812, but for them, too, removal had been inevitable.

In eastern Oklahoma at the turn of the twentieth century, the influx of Anglo-Americans looked down on and discriminated against American Indians, and among the native nations, the Cherokee looked down on the others. Into this stew of grievance and resentment was born Ernest Edwin Evans—one half Cherokee, one quarter Creek, and one quarter white—on August 13, 1908.

His paternal grandfather, George Washington Evans—Ernest's white quarter—had been the mayor of Okmulgee, where he practiced the locally prevalent grift of marrying Native American wives, gaining control of their land, and then divorcing them. He did this to two Creek women, the second of whom bore him a son,

William Charles Evans, whom the senior Evans disinherited along with his other children. The son settled into a laboring life in Muskogee, about two-thirds of the way to Tahlequah, and married a Cherokee named Anna Birdsong, Ernest's mother.

Mostly, the Evans family followed work: While Ernest was still a baby, the family returned for a time to Okmulgee, where William Charles had opened a restaurant. Oklahoma was in an oil boom, there were more white people than ever before, and the town's population had passed two thousand—the prospects were good. The Evanses lived in a two-room house on Main Street, very near the two-story stone Creek capitol, the Council House. They had friendly neighbors, and although their circumstances were modest, the family was happy and grew with the addition of a daughter, Gladys, and the next year another boy, Johnny.

In 1913, the family relocated to Mulberry, Arkansas, a few miles east of Fort Smith, where two more boys were born, Lee and Albert. Living in the Arkansas River Valley between the Ouachita Mountains to the south and the foothills of the Ozarks to the north gave a wilderness tint to Ernest's childhood. He rambled and learned to fish. Then, in the spring of 1917, William Charles brought the family back to Okmulgee, where he worked for a farmer supporting the war effort and earned as much money as he ever had. The family lived here through 1919, then moved to Muskogee to await Ernest's coming of age, when he would attend public schools there.

At the time, American Indian children usually went to trade schools, but the Evans family had more ambitious plans for Ernest, who was bright and curious and had developed a love of reading. The family, though, found themselves once more in hard times, and Anna's mental health began to crack under the renewed strain of being poor. Home in Muskogee was a shanty by the railroad tracks, and while the younger children made a game of chasing the trains, what became clear to Ernest was that those trains into Muskogee brought from faraway places people—people who had occupations and money to travel—and that he was a poverty-stricken boy with no present and no future. Thoughts of escape began to take shape, perhaps with a naval career.

The family split up. William Charles remained in Muskogee to work, and Anna took the children back to Okmulgee. There, Ernest began what would count as his first year of high school in 1922, in one of the trade schools that American Indians customarily attended. That next summer, however, Okmulgee entered a period of racial strife—with a spate of lynchings and vocal support for the resurgent Ku Klux Klan. Vigorous efforts by the governor to discredit the Klan only emboldened greater defiance and exposed the depth of sympathy that many in the community had for it. In fact, Oklahoma had a deeply racist streak, and it was only two years since the Tulsa Race Massacre, one of the worst race slaughters in American history. The Evans family packed up and returned to Muskogee, which appeared less infected. Indeed, the editor of the *Muskogee County Democrat* published a piece criticizing the men and women who were "being controlled by prejudice and sentiment, bigotry and malice." After that summer of 1923, the Evans family never returned to Okmulgee again.

Muskogee had become a small city whose citizens were mostly white, mostly on the make. The increasingly fragile mental health of Ernest's mother thrust on the teenager more responsibility for his younger brothers and sister. He accepted this role with seeming stoicism, although it pulled him away from his love of reading, dreaming of travel while devouring *National Geographic*, and increasingly, thinking of escape. As his family had planned, Ernest enrolled in the nearly all-white Central High School as a sophomore to get a better education. American Indians were not banned from Central—in fact gifted athletes and scholars were welcome—but naturally the family was concerned that there might be incidents.

It was probably Ernest's mother who impressed upon him her people's adage: *The nail that stands up gets hammered down.* He could be ambitious but must not let it show; he could excel in his studies but must not show off. He should get along with everyone and blend in. The adolescent Ernest took this to heart, for it well described his life and his career. In his youth his facial features were identifiable as Native American, but he was not nearly as dark as many others. He developed an easy smile and an approachable manner, traits that would likely help him avoid trouble in high school.

In fact, Ernest found that social balance and made a success of it. He participated in student government, debated successfully, and was appointed to the Ring and Pin committee, the school yearbook, and the Service Club. As treasurer of the latter organization, Evans budgeted for and hosted affairs to honor the outstanding achievers and organizations of the school. On three occasions Evans gave speeches and discovered a gift for entertaining guests. He was not tall or commanding in presence, but he had a loud voice and he exuded grit. His characterization in the school yearbook showed deference to him: "He has the courage of his convictions."

Despite this success in high school, Evans still dreamed of an escape from Muskogee. His thoughts turned increasingly toward the Navy. It was an uncommon trajectory for an American Indian boy. He could simply enlist, or he could apply to the U.S. Naval Academy at Annapolis, where he could further his education for four years and at the end of them graduate as an ensign and look toward a career as an officer. Appointments to the Academy came through the U.S. Congress, usually upon the recommendations of the different representatives. Evans wrote to his congressman and was turned down. No one had to tell him that there were more than enough sons of rich, well-connected white families to fill the limited number of slots for new plebes.

There was, however, more than one way to get in. Evans left his high school graduation party to go to a recruiter, and within a week, he was off to boot camp with the Oklahoma National Guard. He was free of Muskogee; that was the first step. His initial training went smoothly, though Evans did not like what he saw of the Army and requested a transfer into the active Navy, beginning his career in the fall of 1926 as an enlisted sailor.

The Navy was aware that quite apart from the sons of the privileged, there were a number of youths with intelligence, gumption, and resourcefulness who could be a credit to the service, and they held a certain number of slots at Annapolis for those who won a competition among the common seamen. This was one endeavor where being an American Indian didn't stymie Evans: All branches of the service were open to American Indians who wanted to serve. Despite generations of shabby treatment at the government's hands, many had a strong sense of patriotism and felt that military service could redeem their perceived shame at earlier defeat and being sent to reservations.

Evans learned of the Naval Academy preparatory school in San Diego, from which top students left to attend the Academy. After recommendation from his superiors, Evans was admitted, and months later he outscored more than sixty applicants on the admissions test. He missed only two of the multiple-choice questions. To one—"A meal must include?" The correct answer was *Food*. Evans answered *Hunger*. To the other—"A contest always has?" The correct answer was *Opponents*. Evans answered *Victory*. They were wrong answers, but good ones, revealing ones.

CHAPTER 2

Achieving His Dream

JUNE 1931–APRIL 1937

Annapolis at last. Behind the main entrance, walkways of white granite stretched through elm trees and across perfectly kept lawns. Each morning Evans smelled and breathed the air and knew he was near water. The ocean—or at least, the Severn River as it emptied into Chesapeake Bay—was just behind his dorm; an average center fielder could throw a stone to it. In the mornings, rather than swim, Evans assumed the push-up position, staring down at the dirt on the parade ground and reciting facts and lore from the lives of earlier Navy men. Annapolis is the birthplace of modern naval teaching and the Bancroft Hall complex, the dorm that houses all midshipmen, is the largest on the campus.

At the heart of it all lay the chapel, and beneath the chapel in a magnificent tomb, elevated in an elaborate sarcophagus of white-veined Royal Pyrenees black marble, lay the astonishingly preserved body of John Paul Jones, the father of the American Navy.

Nearby, inscribed for all to read, were his words: "I wish to have no connection with any ship that does not sail fast, for I intend to go in harm's way."

From sunrise to sunset Evans worked, knowing now he was a fighter and wanting to prove it. The story in his family was that each member of his father's line had fought in an American war, and now he had a chance to leave his mark. At the Academy, he played football for three years before turning to wrestling and the equestrian competitions of gymkhana—and when not competing, he took to the ruck trails, hiking with a weighted pack on his back. And as every midshipman is given a name to be known by and his American Indian heritage was well known, he became "Big Chief," or "Chief" for short, and sometimes "Cherokee." He found that his heritage earned him respect where he had not expected to find it. By his last year, the editor of the Academy's yearbook wrote that Evans had "endeared himself in the heart of every midshipman."

One thing he was not, however, was a brilliant student. He was in the top half of the class in only a handful of disciplines. Rather, it was the relationships that he built that made impressions on his classmates. As the 1931 *Lucky Bag* noted, although Evans was "endowed with an exceptionally brilliant mind, he advocates and practices a minimum of study and a maximum of reading and pleasure. This policy has enabled him to develop a shining personality and pleasant nature, together with a knowledge of psychology, religion, philosophy, love, or most any subject about which one desires to converse." His highest marks his junior year were in language studies and, his senior year, in aptitude for service. The philosophy of life that he was developing had already come to serve him well, replacing the disadvantages and frustrations of his past with a new motto: *Life is what one makes of it.*

Through his four years at Annapolis, Evans grew more open about his preference for reading, or competition, or fitness, or camaraderie, over study. When he graduated on June 4, 1931, ranked 322 in a class of 443, it was no surprise—especially since he had found an entirely new distraction. Her name was Margaret Wilfong, of Kentucky. They had met at a social event and begun dating seriously through the summer of 1929 while Evans was between semesters.

Countless Navy wives over the years have carped that their husbands married the Navy as well as them but few could say, as Margaret could, that the competition began on the same day. They were wed on Evans's graduation day, and he walked his bride beneath the traditional arch of sabers.

Taking a travel stipend from the Navy, they took a five-day cross-country train trip, honeymooning virtually en route to Evans's first posting at the Naval Air Station San Diego. Their timing was fortunate; the stock market crash a year and a half before had plunged the country into a calamitous depression. Even making their home in spartan military housing on an ensign's pay, they were lucky. Millions now found themselves living the kind of life Evans had left behind in Muskogee—or worse. His past, crowded with wants and worries, disappeared further behind him, and he was glad to see it go. As his granddaughter recalled, "He never visited his family in Oklahoma after he joined the Navy."

Evans even found a new kind of freedom in the cockpit of his Vought VE-7 Bluebird trainer, a stocky, two-seat biplane that first flew in 1917. The return of peace had prompted the Army to cancel their order for a thousand of them, but the Navy developed it into their first fighter plane, covering over the first seat and fitting on a Vickers machine gun, which was synchronized to fire through the propeller. More than a hundred VE-7s were built, one of which made naval history as the first plane to take off from an aircraft carrier.

Something about naval aviation failed to catch fire with Evans, though. And having shown that it was difficult for him to feign interest where it did not lie, he washed out with a notation of his poor grades and disinterest. He had lasted a month and a day, but he refused to despond. Margaret had become pregnant almost at once; they moved to Los Angeles for reassignment and looked forward to the future.

Evans's optimism was well-founded, as he was assigned to the largest and most powerful warship in the Navy, the USS *Colorado*. Margaret and he took up residence only a few blocks from the navy yard. She found a job as a nurse at the local hospital until her pregnancy restricted her, and he began an affair with his magnificent mistress.

The queens of the fleet in 1931 were still the battleships. They had been the focus of the arms race between Germany and the United Kingdom that led up to World War I. Through this time the United States kept pace distantly, hoping to stay out of the coming war. As the British and German navies deployed bigger and bigger guns—from twelve-inch to thirteen-and-a-half-inch, to fourteen-inch, to fifteen-inch rifles—the United States trumped them all when it laid down the *Colorado* in 1919, the first in the world to mount sixteen-inch guns that had half again more punch than the fourteen-inch guns. The *Colorado*-class battlewagons were the last to be completed before the restrictions of the Washington Naval Conference took effect, limiting the size of future Great Power battleships. Therefore *Colorado* and her sisters, *Maryland* and *West Virginia*, were the largest ships in the fleet (and remained so until 1940) and were still the latest expression of battleship design.

Ensign Evans knew all this when he was assigned to the *Colorado* on August 5, 1931. Battleships were the common first duty for new ensigns, because they could be trained in greater numbers in a greater variety of tasks. Later they were distributed to smaller vessels, and the lessons were applicable on them. Adjustment to sea duty was hard for many, but there was one problem Evans did not have. Many junior officers found the conditions cramped, but to Evans, who had shared a bedroom with four younger siblings, the accommodations were downright luxurious.

Colorado—more than two hundred yards long and displacing thirty-three thousand tons, with thousands of compartments— was a fertile training ground. Where a ship of her prestige often performed diplomatic missions and goodwill visits, during the early months of Evans's tenure, *Colorado* stayed close to her home port. The most exciting event was gunnery practice, with the blinding flashes and thunderous roars of her sixteen-inch broadsides. Evans was still new aboard when a five-inch gun of the secondary battery exploded, killing five and injuring twenty-two—a chilling reminder of the danger inherent in handing such deadly weapons.

Life on land went on as usual, however, and Ernest Evans Jr. was born January 24, 1932, but this family time was cut short by the Navy. One month later, the *Colorado* was ordered to Hawaii to participate in coordinated fleet exercises. They were termed "fleet problems," and on his first one, Evans witnessed the ponderous ballet of a gracefully maneuvered task force: seven battleships, three cruisers, and twenty-five destroyers billowed across miles of ocean, with the officers studying plans for a mock battle. It was Evans's first prolonged cruise, allowing him to find his sea legs and trade stories with other officers. He could have told them anything about his life in Oklahoma, for many Easterners' only frame of reference for American Indians came from movies, and they pictured them still on horseback, in beads and feathers and war paint.

When the force arrived at Pearl Harbor, they were met by landing craft to practice amphibious assaults, seventeen submarines to make mock torpedo runs, and one hundred planes. Significantly, the fleet problems included air defense at sea. For years, senior officers had scoffed at the idea that little airplanes could sink a mighty battleship with bombs, even after General William "Billy" Mitchell proved them wrong by sinking the captured German SMS *Ostfriesland* in a demonstration aerial attack in 1921. By 1932 the Navy considered it at least prudent to prepare for the possibility. Off the coast of Oahu, the planes did their best to strike the vessels with simulated bombs, their occasional hits revealed by mounds of white flour that then had to be hosed clean.

In their mock surface battle, Evans found himself inspired by the sight of the mighty sixteen- and fourteen-inch guns swung out and trained in unison, their shattering salvos arcing out toward the imaginary enemy. The seamen gained valuable practice in working as a team, especially in supporting the landing transports as they assaulted a beach—a lesson that would prove to be of particular significance to Evans in later years.

After the opening round of exercises, the sailors began obtaining shore liberty. Pearl and Honolulu were celebrated for the pleasures they offered visiting seamen, and when they mixed with the resident Army troops, things were bound to get raucous. Evans partook, but this was not yet his Navy. He was learning from those it still belonged to. Among the beach crowd were some who had been trained by the generation that had fought the Spanish in the Philippines three decades before. Evans knew his place. Back then junior officers who stepped out of line could end up facedown in the street or be thrown overboard.

The *Colorado* sailed back to California one month after leaving, but before docking, a second "invasion" was performed. Two hundred miles from shore, the force Evans was cruising with split up, attempting to deceive a defending picket line of seventy-one submarines and surface vessels. After a couple of hours, Evans and the thirty thousand men of the attacking force were "sunk." Once ashore Evans was free to go, but the admirals were left to sweat over their mistakes.

━━━

On June 14, 1932, several months after returning from the Hawaiian exercise, Evans descended the gangplank with his duffel bag over his shoulder, then stepped off the *Colorado* for good. His next assignment was a destroyer; he reported four days later to the USS *Roper* (DD-147), one of more than a hundred *Wickes*-class "four-pipers" that had formed the backbone of the U.S. destroyer fleet in the early 1920s. She was an old ship, not so much in age, for she had spent eight of her thirteen years in mothballs, but in design philosophy. Three hundred fourteen feet long and only a thousand ninety tons, lightly armed with four four-inch guns, she mounted a fearsome twelve twenty-one-inch torpedo tubes for disrupting enemy battle fleets. Evans became one of her complement of 101.

It was an adjustment, after nearly a year on one of the Navy's proudest vessels, to come aboard one of the least, which housed one-sixth of the crew of the *Colorado*. *Roper* hung around the West Coast through the New Year, allowing Evans time with his family. Evans was home for the birth of his second son—Jerry David Evans—on January 3, 1933. Margaret was not pleased when he left again weeks after the birth to participate in another set of fleet problems, but she had known the lot of Navy wives when she married him.

In this new set of exercises, the fleet attacked San Francisco and Los Angeles, resulting in useful improvements to the cities' defenses. Evans's deployment on the *Roper* was only for two weeks; he disembarked for the final time on July 1, 1933, and transferred to her sister ship USS *Rathburne* (DD-113). (*Roper* went on to her own small share of fame as the first U.S. warship to sink a German submarine in World War II. In the wee hours of April 14, 1942, off the Bodie Island Lighthouse of North Carolina's Outer Banks, she barely avoided a torpedo from the surfaced *U-85*, gave chase, and sent her to the bottom with gunfire.)

Aboard the *Rathburne*, Evans was in charge of about a dozen enlisted sailors, though she rarely left port before Evans was reassigned yet again. Two months later he detached and was sent again to try his hand in aviation, this time across the continent at Naval

Air Station Pensacola. Barely packed, Evans, Margaret, and the two baby boys were on the train from California to Florida, where he reported on August 13 for training as a student navigator. It lasted eight months. Perhaps stung by his previous washout, Evans tackled the new assignment with zeal, his mind set on getting it right. With an instructor at the controls, Evans was graded on navigation and communication, and as he traversed the increasing air traffic over western Florida, he learned to handle the pressure.

This time, at the end of his training, he succeeded and was assigned to a scouting squadron aboard the cruiser USS *Pensacola*. Only four years old, she presented a daring new design with ten eight-inch guns that super-fired three over two, both fore and aft. In her waist, between the stacks, were fitted a catapult, two biplanes with pontoons for water landings, and a crane for lifting them out of the water. Evans was given a staff role until he acquainted himself with the personnel, equipment, and routines. Once he began flying, he discovered a whole new exhilaration while being slung off a catapult and praying that he reached airspeed before gravity had its wet way with him. Evans also knew that his role was important. The year before, the Navy's failed attempt at "invading" California would have ended differently if they had been able to deploy spotter planes.

In the spring of 1934, the *Pensacola* was given the new home port of Norfolk, Virginia, and after flight school, Evans had a month to move his family there. At least in Norfolk, Margaret would have the advantage of a larger community of other *Pensacola* wives. As they unpacked in Virginia, Evans was called for additional training at the Ford Instrument Company on Long Island,

New York. There he studied the Ford Company's new antiaircraft gun director. In a naval battle he would need to understand the equipment that was feeding enemy coordinates to the cruiser's gunners.

On June 15, 1934, after training in New York, Evans reported to his squadron and was promoted to lieutenant, junior grade (jg). Then came six more months of training to become proficient in aerial observation. In addition, he needed to understand the ship's catapult system, the pilots who flew the aircraft, the men who maintained them, and the gunners whose fire he would be directing.

On January 15, 1935, the *Pensacola* changed home ports again to San Diego. Margaret got a further lesson in being a Navy wife; as Evans transited the Panama Canal, Margaret, caring for the children alone, took the train back to California.

Two weeks after arriving in San Diego, Evans finally began flying from one of the two floatplanes stored amidships. From May 3 to June 10, *Pensacola* participated in a new set of fleet problems, and it was a vast exercise, bounded by Alaska on the north and Hawaii on the south. Fifty thousand sailors in one hundred seventy-seven ships and nearly five hundred planes trained across the vastness of the Northeast Pacific.

The maneuvers aroused more than the usual interest. Japan and the United States were in growing competition. The *Pensacola*'s patrol aircraft, as well as the others operating from the battleships and heavy cruisers of the formation, had an opportunity to scout for the "opposition" two thousand miles east of the threat they were training to fight. From the sky Evans saw battleships in two parallel columns steaming in line ahead, each column stretching several miles. During periods of gunnery practice, the big guns of the battleships came alive, sending three-quarter-ton shells erupting from thunderheads of cordite smoke and spreading sea-flattening shock waves. With clipboard in hand, Evans practiced navigation, looking up at intervals to get his bearings and marking out coordinates from where an attack could come. At low altitude, moving by at almost two hundred miles per hour, he could make out the faces of peers aboard his own ship.

With the end of fleet exercises, Evans returned to San Diego, and for the remainder of 1935, the skies above Southern California were his office, while down below the *Los Angeles Times* covered the *Pensacola*'s boxing team when one of her crew qualified for an amateur card in the city.

In the spring of 1936, the fleet again drilled, this time near the Panama Canal Zone. The work was long, but in one instance, naval tradition demanded its due. Every time a seaman passes below the equator for the first time, he is initiated by gaudy and vaguely lewd rites into the ranks of seasoned sailors. "Pollywogs" are turned into "shellbacks." In this vast fleet, thirty thousand sailors traversed the equator and participated in the largest-ever "crossing the line" ceremony, and this time Lieutenant Evans was one of them.

In the ceremony, rank is forgotten for a few hours, and one seaman, a shellback who has undergone the treatment before, becomes the most powerful man aboard in the guise of King Neptune. May 19, 1936, the night before the ceremonies, Evans received a subpoena, which was slid underneath his door. Its contents stated that come morning he would report to the bow of the *Pensacola* for trial. The Royal Court would be the jury, and the mob

of shellbacks his executioner. The senior most enlisted man—
Davy Jones, wearing grimy overalls and draped in seaweed—
served as the judge. His verdict was unfailingly "guilty."

Ninety-eight ships, some within one hundred yards of one
another, participated in the trial of pollywogs this morning. Each
ship had its own Royal Court, its own King Neptune, and its own
Royal Baby. The Royal Baby was played by the fattest man on the
ship, and a popular punishment was for the uninitiated to kiss the
navel of the Royal Baby—though first, the baby applied a mixture
of vinegar, diesel fuel, and motor oil to his torso.

One of the ninety-eight King Neptunes that day got so drunk
that he was unable to deliver his farewell speech. Instead, he stood
up on deck repeating, "I am satisfied." The Royal Barber, wearing
a white doctor's coat, shaved each pollywog completely bald, only
leaving a few millimeters of hair if officers pleaded to let a pollywog remain presentable for meetings. The clean-shaven pollywogs crawled through a gauntlet of shellbacks who wielded
shaving cream, fish guts, paddles, and high-pressure water hoses.
Officers were offered a way out by paying tribute in beer, but
Evans was no prude, so he endured what the common sailors had
to. That night, the serious war exercises continued as if Davy
Jones's ninety-eight apparitions of his Royal Court had never
walked among the crews.

Once home, Evans returned to a normal cycle, spending a
week or two each month with his family. The Evanses were allowed to remain in San Diego as 1936 closed. His children were
not old enough to know the pain of his absence, but by the spring
of 1937, Evans was expecting new orders. His wife naively hoped
that these would have him work near home.

CHAPTER 3

Manila Days and Isolationism

APRIL 1937–DECEMBER 1941

In the middle of April 1937, Lieutenant (jg) Evans detached from Scouting Squadron Nine. His new assignment was the fleet tug USS *Algorma* stationed in San Diego, though four days later a shuffle of the deck had him swapping over to the troop transport USS *Chaumont*, thirteen thousand tons, sixteen years old, capable of conveying thirteen hundred troops at a time. The Evans family, living in San Diego, found themselves moving to San Francisco after the abrupt change in orders.

Events in China had caught the president's eye. In Shanghai, the Fourth Marine Division oversaw a contested peace. Ships like the *Chaumont* brought Marines to protect American nationals living in the area. On the *Chaumont*, Evans served for a year, from May 3, 1937, to May 27, 1938. He was too junior to request more appealing orders. The foreign experience offered by a deploying troop transport, it was decided, was what Evans's career needed.

Before taking him aboard at San Diego, *Chaumont* transited the

Panama Canal, and Caribbean barnacles still clung to her worn, streaked hull when Evans stepped aboard. The *Chaumont* arrived at Shanghai on July 11, 1937, and remained for three days. At anchor the high-sided, four-hundred-fifty-foot-long transport stood out against the nimble wooden sampans and small vessels of the commercial traffic. The city was in turmoil, as Japan had invaded China four days earlier.

The crew received time ashore, one portion at a time. The spices, clothes, currency, and literature would be novelties at home. On the return journey, these goods, intended for children, wives, and girlfriends, traded hands as men sought to pass the time. At night the hum of snorers and night talkers meshed, and each day the collective smell of the Marines on board grew stronger. In response, the Marines turned *Chaumont* into an acronym: *Christ Help All Us Monkeys On Navy Transports.*

The *Chaumont* arrived back in San Diego on August 27, but Evans had less than two days with his family. His children received gifts and sea tales while the boys, now five and four years old, gave in exchange details of their lives in children's prattle that meant the world to their father.

After *Chaumont*'s departure, tragedy hit Shanghai in August while Evans was en route back to the United States. The Japanese cruiser *Izumo* was anchored near a populated entertainment district that acted as a massive human shield. On the ground, Chinese forces were being overwhelmed, and in desperation Chinese pilots made an attempt on the ship while thousands of civilians were gathered and hidden among the grand markets and theaters of this coastal district. Chinese planes dove, but typhoon-strength winds pushed their bombs off course and into their own people.

Over the next several days, families struggled to find their relatives among nearly one thousand dead.

Evans laid eyes a second time on the mouth of the Yangtze River on September 18, 1937. After a hard turn to port, the transport entered the Huangpu River, which flowed south of the larger Yangtze and marked the eastern boundary of Shanghai. In the middle of the Huangpu, an eighth of a mile wide at her fattest, *Chaumont* dropped anchor. Smoke in the distance marked recent conflicts, and infrequent gunfire marked the cadence of battle outside the city.

The air smelled of fresh-caught fish and fuel oil, but also of burned buildings and sweat. The nationalities with interests in Shanghai were leaving. Evans saw Italian and French destroyers laid at anchor in two rows, straddled throughout the day by hundreds of fishing vessels and barges. The larger ships did not move as the fishermen went about their lives as if an empire had not landed its armies on their shore and was waging war nearby.

The power in Japan lay in the hands of warlords as a liberal civilian government clung to nominal authority. In 1931 militarists at the country's core were victorious in throwing off the restrictions of the Washington naval treaty, and a massive naval buildup began in secret. Now, in the summer of 1937, the next part of *Japan's Reconstruction Program* to unfold was the consolidation of gains made in China. This plan was written out by a famous Japanese philosopher two decades before, and was essentially the Japanese *Mein Kampf*.

This empire, smaller than California, possessed seventy million people, who were worried about their place in the world after the United States and Great Britain snubbed their citizens in immigration status and imposed harsh restrictions on their ship-building. The West tried their hardest to ignore the fact that Japan was an expansionist and imperialist power that had soundly defeated China in a war in 1894–1895, and Russia in 1904–1905 in a war that had given Korea to Japan as a sphere of influence and that saw the Russians surrender half of Sakhalin Island to Japan. Based on many years of successful conquest, the Japanese military leadership grew more assertive toward the moderate civilian leaders they worked alongside.

Evans left Shanghai a second time on September 22 and reached the Golden Gate again on December 15, 1937. Hoots and hollers quickly boiled up within the ship, and as many sailors as could fit on deck clamored to greet the new bridge that had been finished mere months before.

Evans knew that peace was crumbling, but back home with his wife and sons, he was able to welcome the New Year with a smile. When he returned to Shanghai on February 11, 1938, he held to these memories to offset the hell he found.

Two months before, Japanese troops had slaughtered hundreds of thousands of people in Nanking, prompting the realization that it was time for Americans to get out. On December 11, the river gunboat USS *Panay* was evacuating U.S. diplomats from the consulate in Nanking when three Japanese bombers attacked. *Panay* was sunk and three Americans were killed in what was probably a deliberate attempt by the Japanese to draw the United States into the conflict, as American retribution would have given the Japanese military leaders the pretext to silence the moderates in their government.

Chaumont left China filled with angry Marines on February 18,

1939. It was Evans's third port call in China, and he detached at the end of May, remaining unassigned through the end of June. Evans was due a rest, and on June 30, 1938, he was given command of the USS *Cahokia*, a harbor tug assigned to the Mare Island naval facility in the northern reaches of San Francisco Bay.

As had come to be his habit, Evans was good-humored about being the captain of a harbor tug. It was a small job, but he could not beat the life it afforded him. Home was less than three miles away, and the *Cahokia* never left San Francisco Bay. The job lasted for a year and a half, until Evans detached from his responsibilities as captain on June 10, 1940. In the time since taking command, he had been promoted to lieutenant and strengthened his record, exhibiting disciplined leadership over twenty men. Operating on a schedule of two weeks on and two weeks off, Evans was often home with his family. He became a common sight at the Bay Area fish markets, restaurants, and grocery stores, as well as at his children's elementary school. At times, life felt ordinary, but through their social circles, the couple continued to hear stories of Japanese atrocities in China.

It could not last. Evans returned to the fleet in the fall of 1940, assigned to the Asiatic veteran USS *Black Hawk* (AD-9), a destroyer tender of fifty-nine hundred tons. He had two months to consider the irony of being assigned to a ship named for a war chief of the Sauk Nation, and during those two months, he prepared to leave for duty in the South China Sea while his family resettled in Long Beach. In the summer of 1940, Manila saw an increase in attack subs stationed there and a related increase in destroyers used to escort them. This promised to be a busy posting.

As a senior lieutenant, Evans was named the ship's gunnery

officer. The *Black Hawk* was in Tsingtao, China, at the time Evans received the assignment, but he joined the ship at Manila, where he arrived on September 15, 1940. Each of her four five-inch gun mounts, presented boldly at the ship's corners, had a crew and backup of four, plus two ammunition handlers. These crews were likely taken aback by a new officer who wanted to learn all the intimacies of the guns and their operation in short order.

A destroyer tender was a mobile maintenance base and supply vessel. She carried some ammunition and depth charges, and maintained a fully equipped machine shop that could make any repair a destroyer would need short of dry-docking. Among the crew were even clockmakers who could repair sextants and chronometers. *Black Hawk* was assigned to Destroyer Squadron 29, which had been subdivided into Divisions 57, 58, and 59—each with four, four, and five destroyers, respectively. Tenders like *Black Hawk* were assigned to the squadron overall, but serviced the divisions as they maneuvered around the Philippines, completing patrol assignments. For three months she cruised the Philippines with the squadron before being relieved by another tender and committing herself to Manila Bay on December 19, 1940.

Evans remained in this duty through April 1941. The ship's boxing team helped cure boredom and it was an activity that Evans encouraged, but he learned that he needed greater separation from his men. Aside from boxing, they devised an impromptu form of hockey, although keeping the puck—usually a flattened can of beans—on the deck was tough. At night, movies were projected onto bedsheets hung from the ship's superstructure. Evans took roll at 0800 muster on the quarterdeck. With the men prey to tropical pleasures, absentees were either hungover in their berths, hungover in jail, or gone with a girl. The punishment was a two-week sentence to the ship's brig, and the prisoner was restricted to limited water and food except every third day. The commander in chief of the Asiatic Fleet, Admiral Thomas C. Hart, looked with disdain on the Philippines and regarded the Navy base in Manila as more or less a penal colony. Hart's opinion was not without reason, but Lieutenant Evans led first through his own good example in expecting his gun crews to stay out of trouble.

After nearly four months of inactivity, the *Black Hawk* weighed anchor for a patrol on April 7. The squadron refueled and traveled to the southern Philippine ports of Davao and Zamboanga City— important ports to the Spanish in previous centuries. Evans's gunners still did not have much to do. On occasion a fishing vessel got too close and Evans fired a shot across her bow, but aside from this, all Evans needed to do was perform routine inspections of his powder. While Japan was preparing for war, Evans was aboard the *Black Hawk* trying sailors at captain's mast—an informal judicial hearing—for drinking from stores of bootlegged alcohol.

In July 1941, the ever-expanding Japan completed its capture of French Indochina. In response, on July 26, President Roosevelt froze all Japanese assets in the United States. This silenced the remaining moderates in Japan and put the warlords' plans in full motion. The Japanese war machine, however, needed oil, and that could be secured only from the Dutch East Indies. War planners realized that a strike there required neutralizing any possible retaliatory action, and that—they no longer caught their breath when they discussed it—meant the elimination of the United States Pacific Fleet at Pearl Harbor.

Meanwhile, Evans's reputation was rising in the squadron. He was popular with his crews despite his meting out strict punishment. Ship captains came to know the *Black Hawk*'s gun boss as a reliable sailor and a strong-willed junior officer. His worldliness and tough upbringing began to show, and his experience in the South China Sea proved valuable. It was felt that if he were needed, he could command.

In the summer of 1941, the destroyer *Stewart* of Division 58, a fighting ship, needed a capable lieutenant. At that time, that division was operating in the southern Philippines. *Black Hawk* left Manila on July 31, and by the afternoon of August 3 had covered seven hundred miles to reach Tawi-Tawi, at the very southwestern corner of the Philippines near Borneo. Here Evans detached from the *Black Hawk* and came aboard the heavy cruiser *Houston*, which aimed to bring him to the *Stewart* for duty. This order, though, did not stand. Instead, the *Houston* carried Evans to the USS *Alden*, (DD-211), a destroyer in need of an executive officer.

The *Black Hawk* had worked closely with every ship of the squadron, and everyone understood that the tender's zealous gunnery officer was an underused fighter. Word had passed among the commanders in the squadron that *Alden* needed a second-in-command. Evans's name was discussed, and he was chosen. As exec he was responsible for setting the daily schedule, interacting with the chief petty officers, managing the ship's supplies, and serving as the right hand to the captain, Lieutenant Commander L. E. Coley. *Alden* was another flush-deck four-piper, but two hundred tons heavier and a step up in design from the *Roper* vintage.

Confident that he was the right man for the job, Evans dove headfirst into getting the *Alden*'s crew into fighting shape. His days became encompassed with managing the hundred-ten-man crew of mechanics, cooks, gun men, torpedomen, lookouts, navigators, radio room and boiler room men, and yeomen. For the next couple of months, Evans honed them into condition, his gunners' mates soon able to spit out a four-inch shell every eight seconds and his firemen able to gear up in under a minute.

On November 24, Admiral Hart handed down orders for the *Black Hawk* and four destroyers to receive fuel at Balikpapan, an oil port on the east coast of Borneo. The orders were to go to the Dutch for fuel but to claim that they were having "difficulty" in obtaining it. This plan was insurance for the destruction of oil supplies, should the Dutch refuse to destroy them in the face of a Japanese attack.

The movement to Borneo was uneventful and *Alden* spent ten nights at Balikpapan before new orders came on December 5. The fading light backlit *Alden*'s knifelike hull, and her four distinct stacks cast a shadow on the water. In the ship's wardroom, Evans and his captain scratched their heads, trying to make sense of the facts.

Admiral Hart continued to express confidence that Japan could not defeat the United States. The Asiatic Fleet was small, but the Pacific Fleet was only days away. Destroyer Squadron 29 represented nearly the entire offensive might of the Asiatic Fleet, and its three destroyer divisions were being pulled apart. There were three dated cruisers, but these were widely spread. The submarines could fight, too, but after hostilities began, supply lines would quickly be cut.

On the afternoon of the fifth, Evans and Commander Coley learned that during conferences in Manila earlier that day, the British Admiralty had asked Hart to send a division of destroyers to contribute to the vanguard of two Royal Navy battleships in Singapore. Evans, the *Alden,* and the rest of DesDiv 57 were anchored at Balikpapan; Division 58 was at Tarakan, another vital Bornean oil port more than five hundred miles north; and Destroyer Division 59 was at Manila. The question of an attack was more a matter of when than of where. The Japanese needed to destroy Manila in order to reach Borneo, and they needed to neutralize Singapore to capture Java.

In the days leading up to the attack on Pearl Harbor, the immediate Allied naval concern was their dearth of destroyers. Four had come down with the British battleships but more were wanted. Hart hesitated to deliver his destroyers to the British, as no officer wants to surrender resources to another chain of command. On December 6, word came from Singapore that a Japanese amphibious expedition had been sighted in the Gulf of Thailand. Evans had already spoken with his enlisted chiefs by the morning of December 7. They knew to expect a movement order. Hours after sunrise, more reports confirmed a Japanese presence and that prodded Hart to action. Division 57 was sent toward Singapore that morning. In the waning hours of peace, Ernest Evans was the most senior lieutenant and second-in-command aboard a fighting ship.

CHAPTER 4

Son, We're Going to Hell

DECEMBER 1941–FEBRUARY 1942

Before departing Balikpapan, Evans learned of Japanese air activity to the north. Seventy-two hours before war began, American pilots on coastal patrol from Manila made eye contact with Japanese pilots. As Evans waited below the clouds at Balikpapan, the opposing pilots circled one another, avoiding conflict.

The news was ordinary—Japanese pilots had been flying from Taiwan for months, but Evans decided that it would be good to alert his junior officers and chiefs. The maintainers in the engine room, the men next on watch, and his gunners serving under them needed an understanding of the gravity of this voyage. They were about to leave Balikpapan, the largest oil port on Borneo's east coast, and travel to Singapore.

They meant to leave the morning of December 7; however, the Dutch wouldn't raise their anti-submarine nets until nightfall, hesitant to let Americans abuse their strict harbor management. Evans's nerves, certainly taut, were given slack when he learned that they would be leaving Balikpapan under cover of night after all. After hours, from the bridge, he saw his ship clear of Balikpapan harbor. They moved east out of that inlet, then south. Off to starboard, Borneo was illuminated by a waning gibbous. As the moon sank, the coastal mountains were backlit, presented as a shadowy ridge shifting in depth but not in shape above a dense jungle that was hidden by the dark.

The ships proceeded south in column. It was about nine on the night of December 7, but the destroyer could not make full steam because it was strapped down by escort responsibility. The crew positioned the ship in an anti-submarine disposition around the destroyer tender *Black Hawk* and cut the water at fifteen knots. The majority of the crew was asleep except for the diligent, steely-eyed lookouts who were finishing out the first watch of the night.

The only light was that moon. Each ship in the convoy was practicing strict no-light orders. Under the nearly full moon, the outlines of the guns on the *Black Hawk* were visible. Singapore was nearly four days away at this pace. Ordered there for supplies and liberty, the crew would get time ashore while the British forces gathered.

At 0105, GMT + 8—fifty minutes before the first wave attacked Hawaii—the *Black Hawk* was ordered to Surabaya, a major naval base on the eastern shore of Java, Dutch East Indies. The oil was needed at that rear echelon outpost. In the event of war, it would be the last bastion to fall.

Once rid of their escort duty, the four destroyers increased steam pressure and pushed on at twenty-five knots. The *Alden* lurched forward and assumed an even pace, her two screws putting out just over 26,000 horsepower. Under the waterline, men wrestled with tools to keep the archaic steam engines alive, and soon the lookouts of the second watch relieved those on the first. Before the middle watch came to replace them, the United States had been dragged into World War II.

For Evans it was 0331 on the eighth. In *Alden's* radio room, the message was received: "Japan had started hostilities. Govern yourselves accordingly." Evans was fetched from his cabin. The certainty of war erased any uncertainties from when he had found Commander Coley in the officers' wardroom; now his heart was pounding. The crew awoke to this news.

So great was the disbelief that some took the news to mean that the USS *Oahu*—a small river gunboat—had been attacked. Immediately, the normally laissez-faire attitude that the sailors allowed themselves at Manila vanished and was replaced by vigilance. Each port immediately began implementing blackout policies. Where they had expected to receive a warm embrace, they would now wait and prepare. In two days they would be in Singapore and receive their first war orders.

On the evening of the tenth, Evans made his way to the bridge. The last day of the journey was a particularly nervous one. The ship's small size made it likely that Japanese bombers would either ignore or miss it, but Japanese submarines wouldn't.

The ship approached the dock and Commander Coley ordered the engines to be put on idle several hundred yards from shore. Ships tied neatly to barges were ahead of them, while others tied to the dock beyond got attention from workers and contractors employed by the Royal Navy. Fishing and merchant ships were having their white stacks painted gray after a command from local authorities pressed the empire's commercial arm into service.

Despite all the activity of dockworkers, the British battleships had clearly left with their escorts, so the Americans docked and sent men ashore to collect orders.

The air was thick with activity. Oil workers and British sailors ran along distant docks. The rising staccato of their boot steps reached over the sea. Men with fuel hoses lined the dock to greet them. Once tied up the *Alden* refueled, though the oil flow was cut off twice by air raid alarms. After the second one, Evans learned that the division would head northeast and rendezvous with the battleships.

Minutes after reading these orders, further word came that two British battleships had been targeted by bombers. The order to move was pushed up. Evans halted fueling operations and prepared for a search and rescue under the cover of dark. They had until daybreak on the eleventh or they might face the same threat. Before sunset the *Alden* was steaming in column toward the open Java Sea, though before reaching the open ocean they passed alongside two British destroyers on a divergent course. The HMS *Vampire* and *Express* passed by with hundreds of oil-doused sailors aboard, confirming that at least one of the other battleships had been sunk. By light signal the British confirmed that the *Prince of Wales* and the *Repulse* had both gone down. Evans knew his crew did not think much of sailing into a defenseless position.

Evans's guns could not reach high-altitude threats or respond to any surface threat beyond five miles. His torpedoes were his best weapon, but so early in the war, few targets for them were likely to appear. The air war was the first to start.

At the Naval Academy, Evans had war-gamed conflict in the Far East, though his instructors had assumed that the United

States would have a battleship force to deploy. The attack at Pearl had removed that factor for the Americans. With only three far-flung American cruisers in the Asiatic Fleet, when Evans arrived at the site of the sinking, his destroyer was the largest American ship for hundreds of miles. His sailors might have dozed off during midwatch several months before, but they now stood with backs erect, ears and eyes tuned to the sounds and sights of the midnight sea. All the lights were out. For the fourth night in his service aboard her, Evans did not have to enforce the standing order to report all sailors with nervous smoking habits. He had enlisted sailors to round up those careless ones and supply them with chewing tobacco. Those who got the stashes of chew were happy to surrender their smokes. It was a sign of Evans's growing style as a leader: correcting a situation not with discipline but with a constructive alternative.

Evans heard an impossibly high volume of torpedo reports this night. Before the sun rose on the eleventh, his lookouts reported dozens of disturbances on the water. At night, the officers and men of *Alden* believed them to be misidentified dolphins, but the next morning, they were sobered when a broadcast from Japan declared that thirty-eight torpedoes had been fired at an enemy light cruiser in the Gulf of Thailand. The *Alden* was a destroyer, but her silhouette matched closely enough the *Marblehead* class of light cruiser for this report to have a chilling effect.

Back at Singapore, after finding no survivors on the night of the eleventh, Evans took on fuel and allowed a third of his crew liberty on a four-hour leash. The captain was away at meetings, so the *Alden* was Evans's ship. He ordered repainting of the hull. It was made clear the night before that their peacetime solid gray paint scheme would get them killed. Suspended over the edge by rope, just a dozen sailors accomplished the task in a day.

Evans's break came on the thirteenth when Captain Creighton, an American naval observer in Singapore, invited the skippers and their execs to a club for dinner. It was a nicety of command that Evans could get used to. They looked over the harbor while they ate and talked. When asked about home, Evans was likely honest about his background in poverty, which would have generated a great deal of respect among the group.

While listening to one another's tales, they were disrupted twice by air raid alarms that proved false. The British ships in harbor did not move from anchor and the alarms subsided in minutes. Dinner ended when the destroyer captains received orders from Admiral Hart to report to their ships and recall their crews.

By 0800 on the fourteenth, Evans had taken roll call and gone below to check in with his junior officers. Then they departed for Surabaya, Java. Destroyer Division 57 arrived at 1715 the next evening; at the gates of the port, the crew felt a great deal of gratitude for being a couple hundred miles farther from Japan than they had been.

At Surabaya, the various captains briefed one another on the movements of the fleet and left their executive officers in charge. When Commander Coley returned from his string of meetings, he made sure to fill Evans in. The conferences accomplished a degree of coordination; it became accepted that Manila was lost, and the Allies' sparse resources were unilaterally concentrated on holding Java and Australia.

A line of defense would be set on the Malay Barrier, running east of Surabaya down to Timor. Singapore was not defendable despite British insistence to the contrary. Java was the Allies' northwestern sanctuary. The Allies could escape west toward Iran or southeast toward Australia. Port Darwin, a ramshackle port on Australia's northern coast, rose to importance. From there arms and oil could be run to Java. The *Alden* was chosen to protect this supply line from Japanese submarines.

The USS *Trinity*, just safely returned to Surabaya from Manila, would be the first charge under Evans's care as it transported a National Guard battalion. On the evening of the seventeenth, the *Alden* left Surabaya. The crew would maintain escort responsibilities between Darwin and Java through the end of January 1942. That entire time, the threat of submarine attack never went away, though no attack came. The worst danger came from the weather; on January 12 gigantic waves threatened the *Alden* when she was barely a day out of Darwin. She rolled as much as thirty degrees in the swell while Evans and his captain spent two days on the bridge with hatches sealed—but water filled the bridge through shattered windows anyway.

The same waves threatened to capsize the Army transports with their National Guard troops packed inside. Evans was glad to see these soldiers safe ashore after forty-eight hours of high drama at sea. After this task the *Alden* was going to get into a fight, it seemed, but this first plan made by the combined American, British, Dutch, and Australian naval commands—termed ABDA NavCom—was aborted.

Since hostilities had begun the ABDA military forces struggled to form a cohesive syndicate. The multiple nations used different languages, codes, signals, and methods. However, by

January 20, a plan jelled to send a striking force ahead to attack Japanese shipping at Kema, Borneo, on the island's east coast. One cruiser and four destroyers would attack the port, with the *Alden* held in the rear with the powerful heavy cruiser USS *Houston* to cover the retreat. However, the attack was called off when two Allied submarines scouting the area observed no transports to target. So a day after the *Alden* dropped the national guardsmen off at Surabaya, she was assigned another escort task, and left again for Darwin.

Evans was certainly disappointed, but while traveling south on January 20, just hours from Darwin, lookouts on the other destroyer in the convoy noticed a phosphorescent torpedo wake off to starboard. The white trail, spotted by a lookout on the *Edsall*, approached from the rear and passed within feet. The *Edsall* sent out an alarm and signal light to *Alden* to confirm the sighting. Then a second wake was spotted running parallel eighty yards off to port.

The *Edsall*, in the lead, radioed for the *Alden* to attack. In seconds one hundred men were at general quarters. The ship shuddered as the starboard screw was put in reverse and the port engine turned full ahead. It was a cutting right turn that brought the *Alden* a hundred eighty degrees around. Rubber soles echoed over the steel decking as some of the eight officers and senior chiefs hurried to corral the ninety other sailors aboard. The depth charge racks at the rear of the ship were now called on. The *Alden* made sonar contact at three thousand yards and pursued. The *Edsall* covered the transport while the *Alden* moved in to chase down the sub on the open ocean.

Sinking a submarine is a testament to a captain's skill. Each captain must determine his options well in advance and the matchup can take hours, though the action happens quickly. Evans stood abreast of his captain while the helmsman conned the ship.

Throughout the twentieth, the *Alden* searched and dropped depth charges with no apparent success. Evans stood on the wing of the bridge glaring down the length of the *Alden*, looking for debris, a torpedo track, or the submarine itself. If it had surfaced, Evans's gunners would have had a short window of time to crack her hull before she disappeared. Each of the senior chiefs at those gun mounts knew that their executive officer was watching.

As the night of the twentieth gave way to daybreak on the twenty-first, there was no noise on the bridge, save for the ping of the sonar and the intermittant course changes from the captain. At midday on the twenty-first, the destroyer was forced to refuel at Darwin, but in eight hours, it would be back on the scene and take over the hunt from Australian units that had tracked the sub since midday. By 1900 the Australians had left the *Alden* and *Edsall* to search; each vessel was on opposite ends of a mile-wide oil slick that was suspected of being released by the submarine as a diversion.

They hunted through the night of the twenty-first. That night the crew remained awake for fear that they would drown in their sleep. The oil slick had convinced some that their prey had been sunk, but Evans and his captain did not assume victory. Evans knew that German U-boats in the Atlantic often displayed similar deception by releasing oil.

That night, Evans stood on the bridge listening to the ocean.

Under the cover of darkness, the submarine must surface for air and to recharge batteries, but drop under again before first light on the twenty-second. When the sun rose, the submarine and her crew would again become the hunter.

Shortly after 0700, sonar contact was made at eight hundred yards, bearing one hundred thirty-five degrees. Lookouts craned their necks in that direction while the sonarmen continued to listen to their undersea receiver for signs of life. This was no school of fish; propeller noise from three hundred yards away came through their earphones.

On the stern, men stood by for word from the bridge to launch depth charges. Could they kill a sub? Evidently not. When the order came, a simple mechanical issue jammed the depth charges in place, giving the submarine time to slip underneath the *Alden* and make for the open ocean. One depth charge was able to roll off the track before it jammed, and Evans ran to the opposite rail of the ship in time to watch six undersea explosions register. Clearly their one depth charge had hit.

For two hours Evans hunted independently of the *Edsall*, which was on the opposite end of a growing oil slick. A spotter aircraft joined and guided the *Alden* directly to the submarine; it had surfaced to make repairs. Practiced gunners took aim from a mile off. Through binoculars Evans watched. The submarine, apparently leaking oil, was unable to dive as they closed.

To Evans's surprise several Japanese climbed onto the sub's deck and aimed their single deck gun. The concussion of his own guns rang loud in his ears. The explosion of the submarine shook them as the *I-124* erupted in fire and smoke. Standing on the bridge, Evans must have felt like a real sailor. Below him the men at his gun turret broke out in self-congratulation. His was the first American surface combatant of the war to sink a Japanese submarine.

The long chase and duel with *I-124* off Darwin had proven the Japanese ability to operate in the Timor Sea and Indian Ocean. Now this danger had to be assumed each time the *Alden* weighed anchor from Darwin. After the hunt was finished on the twenty-second, the *Alden* made another trip between Java and Darwin. Then a dispatch on February 2 requested that all units operating under the multinational ABDA command gather at Tjilatjap, Java. By the morning of the third, the *Alden* had left Darwin with *Black Hawk*, *Trinity*, *Holland*, and *Otus* in column behind him.

By the eighth, Evans and his captain received orders for their tankers. Several destroyers and cruisers needed refueling after returning from an operation north of Java. At Tjilatjap, after rendez-vousing and refueling at sea from the tankers Evans had brought from Darwin, this force would recount their experiences against the Japanese.

By the evening of February 10, this force anchored at Tjilatjap. Onshore Evans listened as the sailors of the cruisers *Houston* and *Marblehead* and those of Destroyer Division 58 recalled the actions of the previous two weeks. Evans had not yet exchanged shots with larger ships or faced the hopeless reality of an attack by air, so he listened and read those sailors' expressions, stealing through them a glimpse of his enemy.

Evans would have been particularly interested to hear of the destroyer raid at Balikpapan in which five Japanese transports were sunk from only a thousand yards. And judging by the amount of emergency work being done to the cruiser *Marblehead* as she lay docked, he must have believed that her sailors clearly had a story to tell. Tjilatjap's facilities, however, were not equipped to repair such extensive damage, and *Marblehead* was sent to Iran at half speed a few days after arriving. This was bad because it reduced the cruiser force from two to one; the cruiser *Boise* had already been put out of the fight when it had grounded on a reef. Now with one cruiser, the Americans were expected to contribute even less to the ABDA force's resistance to Japan. The USS *Houston* was the last American cruiser and the only heavy cruiser the ABDA navy had, and her aft eight-inch turret had been disabled by a bomb that struck during the same engagement in which the *Marblehead* had been crippled.

On the tenth of February, the *Houston* was sent toward Darwin, and the *Alden* and *Paul Jones* followed the next day as escorts to several empty tankers. When Evans arrived at Darwin on the seventeenth, the *Houston* was not there. That cruiser docked at Darwin several hours after the *Alden* arrived. Then that cruiser's captain, Albert Rooks, told a story.

Two days before, Rooks had left Darwin with an Army unit bound for Timor, but aircraft attacked him at sea. Rooks's crew shot down seven bombers, but because the Japanese had used a short-range-type aircraft, Rooks determined them to be from a Japanese carrier. The reinforcement mission was aborted immediately.

Now any further movement across the Java Sea was threatened by air attack as well as by submarine or surface vessels. The *Houston* and *Alden* left Darwin together on the afternoon of the seventeenth. Two days later Darwin was attacked by more than two hundred and thirty aircraft. Thirteen Allied merchant ships were destroyed, and the next day, Darwin was abandoned as a naval base.

The *Alden, Paul Jones,* and *Houston* arrived in Tjilatjap on the evening of the twenty-first of February. As they approached that entrance, Dutch antiaircraft gunners positioned to guard the harbor strafed a friendly PBY pilot and forced the pilot to make an emergency landing, though not before dropping a depth charge that nearly hit the *Houston.* Then, upon reaching the harbor entrance, the three ships learned that a harbor pilot would not be immediately available to guide them through the minefield.

On the bridge, Evans paced. At that late hour of the Asiatic campaign, Japanese submarines were likely to be stalking. Outside the minefield they were threatened, but after a couple hours' wait, they were guided in at sunset. After this initial disservice, they had to pump their own fuel because the oil company employees had fled.

The following morning, as the cover of night yielded to dawn, Evans was sailing north through the Sunda Strait, bound now for Surabaya. Ominously, before leaving Tjilatjap, a sailor on the *Houston* had asked where they were going—after losing their aft eight-inch turret, they expected to follow *Marblehead* to Iran for repairs—but a senior enlisted replied, "Son, we're going to hell."

Standing on the bridge, Evans saw the entrance to Surabaya harbor an hour before arriving. Dense black smoke had risen from a recently sunk freighter, which was beached onshore outside the minefield. *Alden* made it through, however, and once the ship was anchored, Evans was greeted at the dock by a local quartermaster and supply officers.

A fresh supply of torpedoes came aboard. The handlers acted

quickly, hoping to finish the job before any Japanese planes caught them with explosives exposed on the wharf. As Evans oversaw preparation of the destroyer, his captain was meeting with the overall force commander. Afterward, sitting in the wardroom of the *Alden*, Commander Coley explained to Evans that in a few days their destroyer division would join the other ships around them at anchor on a mission. There were Dutch and Australian cruisers lying about and a British cruiser was expected to join them by the morning of the twenty-second. The target was the easternmost of two Japanese invasion forces that were expected to make landfall on Java's north shore within forty-eight hours. This eastern invasion force was flanked by a covering force estimated at four cruisers and a dozen destroyers. This strength created the need to collect all available ABDA naval power.

On the evening of February 25, Evans set out from Surabaya with the ABDA fleet. They went east to screen the coastline of Madura Island, then shifted a hundred eighty degrees and doubled back to sweep Java's northern coast. However, no Japanese were found. They returned to Surabaya to attempt a sweep the next evening.

At Surabaya on the morning of the twenty-sixth, the USS *Houston* secured her legacy as a serious antiaircraft weapon and overall patron saint of the Asiatic Fleet. Men in noncombat positions could only brace themselves and chain-smoke as the bombs fell. The sailors at the *Houston*'s gun mounts and in her ammo-handling rooms did not get respite, but they brought down seven Japanese bombers. They slept soundly once sunset came. The force went out the night of the twenty-sixth to repeat the sweeping operation, but they were still too early.

Instead, the Japanese found them in the morning as they were reentering Surabaya's harbor. The *Houston* was the first to open fire. Evans watched from the *Alden* as the cruiser shot at three Japanese patrol aircraft that had ducked below the clouds for a look at the state of Surabaya harbor.

From these spotters, reports began landing on the desk of the Japanese officer responsible for the eastern invasion and covering force. Admiral Takeo Takagi was moved to recall his invasion and move in his cover force. It was a cautious reaction to pull off the invasion beach, showing that Takagi believed the Allies had the fighting men and ships to destroy his gathered forces.

The Japanese air patrol correctly related to Takagi the size of the Allied force. At sea, it consisted of three British destroyers— *Electra*, *Encounter*, and *Jupiter*—in a van abreast of one another and leading the other ships. Five miles behind the British destroyers were five cruisers—*De Ruyter*, *Exeter*, *Houston*, *Perth*, and *Java*—six hundred yards apart in column. Seven miles behind the cruisers, also in column, were the four older American destroyers—*John D. Edwards*, *John D. Ford*, *Paul Jones*, and *Alden*. Two additional destroyers, the Dutch navy's *Witte de With* and *Kortenaer*, were off Evans's port side. If the formation had been a constellation in the sky, it would have appeared as a scorpion, though as the battle to come progressed, the formation's makeup would change.

The eastern invasion force was already unloading their sixty transports on the beaches at Kragan, Java, when word came of the ABDA force coming from the east. The Japanese had snuck in behind the ABDA force after Dutch admiral Karel Doorman in *De Ruyter* turned back for Surabaya that morning, but now the enemy fumbled back aboard their transports in response to Takagi's order.

The covering force came in from the northwest. It aimed to interpose between whatever the Allies were bringing and their own transports. The rising sun battle ensigns spanked in the five-knot headwind. The Japanese ships moved ahead at nearly thirty knots in the ten-foot swell. Above it all there was a thick layer of stratus clouds at fifteen thousand feet.

The transports were barely off the beach when at 1612 lookouts on the *Electra* noticed pagoda masts on the horizon to the east. A covering force, under the command of Admiral Takagi himself, was twenty-two miles away and coming to the transports' aid. Each moment more masts were noticed on the horizon, like a winter forest with metal branches continuing to appear. They came in two equal columns parallel to one another: seven destroyers with one light cruiser ahead. The southernmost Japanese destroyer column was headed by the *Jintsu,* and to the north a second column was headed by the *Naka.* Farther west, ahead of these two columns, were two heavy cruisers: the *Nachi* and *Haguro.*

Evans could not see them; the American units were seven miles farther behind the British destroyer van. The initial ABDA shooting would belong to the heavy cruiser *Houston,* whose gunners manually elevated her old rifles and pointed them the old-fashioned way, gunlaying by eyesight. Behind *Houston* the other warships limbered up their turrets and prepared for battle.

The initial shooting started four minutes after the sighting. At 1616 the *Nachi* and *Haguro* began firing on the ABDA cruisers from sixteen miles, or twenty-eight thousand yards. Two red-orange halos illuminated the silhouettes of the two Japanese cruisers before cordite smoke obscured them and a shock wave followed. The large-caliber shells fell almost vertically—plunging fire to penetrate the Allied ships' lightly armored decks—though they fell short. They formed towers of seawater, but vanished into a cloud of mist before the ABDA cruisers. The British destroyers continued on at full steam, not targets because of their small size and swift speed.

The *Houston* was the first ABDA ship to fight, opening up at 1618 at a range of twenty-five thousand yards. The other four ABDA cruisers, carrying only six-inch guns, could not yet cover the gap. The British destroyers were only eleven miles away from the Japanese at the start, but their 4.7-inch guns needed the range to close four more miles. The two forces started the battle on divergent courses, with the Japanese sixty degrees relative to the heading of the ABDA ships, though soon they were running parallel to one another as the Japanese aimed to overtake them.

Evans was far back and unable to respond at the battle's inception. Still, the odds were about even for the outcome. Morale was high, but amid the thunder of the heavy guns, Evans could hear above him Japanese spotter planes that were stealing glimpses at the formation through the cloud cover. The Americans had no such aid.

After three minutes of near misses, the Japanese landed a hit on the leading ABDA cruiser, though the shell failed to explode and exited above the waterline and the *De Ruyter* maintained full speed. If the Japanese had had more heavy guns, they would have inflicted more initial damage because the misses came in clusters. When a hit registered, it was likely that multiple shells would land. It was lucky that the first hit came alone and failed to explode.

Admiral Takagi was heading west by southwest at the start, and the ABDA column west by northwest. To bring his light cruisers into the fight and to close the range for a torpedo attack, Takagi ordered the column headed by the *Naka*—north of the *Jintsu* column—directly south. The *Naka* turned to port, to a southwest heading. Now the distance was closing as the ABDA formation continued northwest, hoping to intercept the transports that were expected to appear on the horizon. The *Jintsu* column aimed to intercept the ABDA column later in the battle, a useful hedge in case the ABDA column was faster than the *Naka* column and cut it off to the west, crossing its T.

However, the *Naka* column moved too fast. At thirty-five knots it would cross the ABDA formation's T. The broadside of the leading light cruiser and each destroyer to its rear would have a shot at the entire line of ABDA ships. Soon this would dawn on Admiral Doorman. Meanwhile the two heavy cruisers fired on the ABDA cruisers and even the *Jintsu,* as it closed on its southwest heading, got shots in on the ABDA cruisers.

By 1620 the range dropped to seventeen thousand yards and Doorman realized his problem. To avoid running through the middle of the *Naka* column, now moments from making a torpedo attack, he shifted twenty degrees to the left, effectively turning his column to port. However, this move hung the three British destroyers—operating on a different radio frequency from the Dutch—off to the right. At 15,700 yards, the British destroyers *Electra* and *Jupiter* had the *Naka* in range.

Meanwhile, unknown to Admiral Doorman in the *De Ruyter,* the Japanese destroyers trailing the *Naka* were making a torpedo run. The *Jintsu* column, still with the heavy cruisers, kept a moderate angle of attack, leaving distance for a torpedo attack later in the battle if needed. The British featherweights kept moving northwest and continued to fight, even after Doorman shifted his column twenty degrees to the left. Luckily, the range had also closed for the ABDA light cruisers and Doorman held a three-to-two advantage in that class. After a four-minute duel at eighteen thousand yards between the ABDA light cruisers and the *Naka* column, this column turned hard to starboard, apparently beaten but in fact retreating strategically after putting more than forty torpedoes in the water.

Through the first turn of the formation, Evans remained with the American destroyers off the port quarter of the cruiser *Java*, the rearmost cruiser. *Alden* and the other three American destroyers had orders to stay with the two slower Dutch destroyers, but Evans and his captain appreciated the dangers of following this order. Should Admiral Doorman order a column turn—it had already happened once—and cruisers and destroyers ahead of them perform a radical left turn to port, then *Alden* and the other American units would run through the middle of the formation, causing disarray and perhaps collisions. Neither Evans nor his captain wanted that in their first fight.

The probability that Admiral Doorman would perform an evasive turn to port was high. The American officers knew that if they had to make an evasive turn, the first sign of this order would be the turn itself. Any orders from Admiral Doorman, aboard the lead ship *De Ruyter*, would have to come by radio from the *Houston*, only after being translated by the American liaison on *De Ruyter* and relayed to the *Houston* by light signal. It was best to avoid the danger of being forced to make a quick decision. So the American destroyers turned up their engines, left the Dutch destroyers behind, and formed up on the disengaged side of the ABDA cruisers, still heading west and taking shots from the heavy cruisers *Nachi* and *Haguro* at long range.

Without waiting, Commander Coley pushed the *Alden* into position alongside the *De Ruyter*—still the lead cruiser—so that should the column turn, they would be in a favorable position to cut in front of it. It was 1640. Minutes before, the seven Japanese destroyers headed by the *Naka*—now retreating north—had fired forty-three long-range torpedoes. This was known not because of a hit but because the torpedoes ran out of fuel and detonated ahead of the ABDA fleet. All the while, the *Naka*'s destroyer column laid smoke, which blinded the ABDA formation to the movement of the *Jintsu* column, which still headed southwest and, at a distance beyond ten miles, was out of range of the ABDA light cruisers. The gunners perched in the *Houston* were the only ABDA men never to lose sight of the second Japanese destroyer column. Without a spotter plane, Doorman on *De Ruyter* went blind as more smoke was laid by the *Naka* destroyers at a safe distance. However, the Japanese cruisers benefitted from their own spotter aircraft and shelled at will.

After the *Naka* made her torpedo attack and opened range, the heavy cruisers of the two forces were again the only ships to exchange shots. It was a mistake that Doorman did not turn to starboard and allow his light cruisers to close range. However, his determination to catch the Japanese transports on the open ocean paid off.

Nerves were shot while waiting for the Japanese heavy cruisers to land a hit, but a jolt of hope came before the battle's first hour ended. At 1652 lookouts on the *Houston* spotted the Japanese invasion force over the horizon. Reactively, Admiral Doorman turned from the west to the northwest in an attempt to catch it, but the Japanese officer responsible for the *Jintsu* column anticipated this and maneuvered for a counterattack, turning this column—with the western edge of the ABDA formation—directly south. From twelve miles away, the *Jintsu* and her seven destroyers lined up for their torpedo attack.

The long-range fight continued. By 1655 the *Haguro* was afire and dropped out of the fight. Then Captain Rooks on the *Houston* sighted in the cruiser in front of *Haguro*, the *Nachi*. The *Exeter* fired on *Nachi* also. The *Houston* used red dye in her shells to mark misses, so when red towers began to rise among the misses from the *Exeter*, the sailors on *Nachi* knew they had been found.

For twelve minutes the ABDA formation continued northwest. During this time no hits came, though the circumstances had changed for the worse. By 1707 both the *Naka* and *Jintsu* columns had gained the western edge of the ABDA formation, and to prevent Doorman's advance toward the transports, they cut ninety degrees to the left, turning to port to run in front of him. They were now ten and six miles away, respectively. Fourteen miles to the northwest, the Japanese heavy cruisers followed suit, turning to show their full broadsides.

Doorman's T was not crossed, but it was a dangerous spot. In the next couple of minutes, the Japanese would put another fifty torpedoes in the water. Screaming shells were landing throughout the ABDA formation while Admiral Doorman was weighing his options. At 1708 a shell found its mark, penetrating the British cruiser *Exeter* and igniting a powder chamber underneath the rear gun. Evans was less than one mile from *Exeter* and the heat from that fireball warmed his face and shook the square glass windows of *Alden's* bridge. Abruptly losing half her speed, the *Exeter* turned sharply to the south to avoid a collision with the cruiser *Houston*, which was directly behind her and closing the six-hundred-yard gap.

The *Exeter* was the second cruiser in the column. The ships behind her interpreted her turn as an order to perform simultaneous turns. The *De Ruyter*, ahead of the rest, was busy firing at the closest Japanese destroyers, which were retreating after making a torpedo attack, and did not notice. This cruiser kept straight for six minutes, until turning to rejoin the ABDA column, which turned to copy and then cover the *Exeter* on a southbound heading. Confusion reigned.

The column broke off to port. If Evans had been on the bridge, he would have been appalled by the disarray. On the disengaged side of the cruisers and with his gunners out of range, he was a passive observer to this madness. He was likely disoriented, struggling to keep up with the movements of the column through the smoke. The enemy was too far away. The smoke clouds were thin but getting thicker, building from the fires growing on the *Exeter*. This smoke helped reduce Japanese accuracy at the start of this second hour of shooting, though torpedoes were in the water. At 1715 the Dutch destroyer *Kortenaer* was hit by a single torpedo. It split in two, jackknifed, and sank in less than a minute.

Evans was less than two thousand yards from *Kortenaer*. The image was sickening. She folded in on herself; there were only a few feet between her bow and stern above the water. Then the flames that erupted from her were put out by the sea. The British destroyer HMS *Encounter* fetched 113 survivors, then resumed toward the southeast. The ABDA formation was now retreating, and the *Exeter* was falling behind.

Fortunately the British tin cans *Electra*, *Encounter*, and *Jupiter* dropped steam and stuck with her, falling behind the main body of the ABDA formation. The ABDA force did not slow down, and ten minutes after *Kortenaer* sank, Doorman turned east in full retreat, with the Japanese closing behind. The *De Ruyter*, *Houston*, *Java*, and *Perth* kept the Japanese at a distance with their big guns, while the *Exeter*, a valuable prize, was pursued by three Japanese destroyers and one light cruiser sent to finish her. It is now 1725.

For the next thirty minutes, the ABDA force continued east. Commander Coley had maneuvered *Alden* through the turn from the southwest to the east, allowing the cruisers to take the inner track and form a column on the engaged side. In retreat Evans was on the disengaged side of the cruisers, but from the bridge, he could now observe the fight. The Japanese had closed to within eight miles and the cruisers were firing with their aft guns at them. The *Houston*, whose after turret had been disabled at the Battle of the Flores Sea, was zigzagging to allow her forward turrets to briefly take aim. Their fire was aimed at the cruisers off on the horizon and was not helping in the battle to save the *Exeter* from the four Japanese pursuers, which were under four miles away and closing on the smoke shroud around the *Exeter*.

Evans was abeam the *Houston*, a few hundred yards south as they moved east. On *Alden*, Coley had given his gunners standing orders to fire once the range closed. The range had dropped significantly, and her gunners would have been able to hit the Japanese destroyers that had recently launched torpedoes at them, but the

Houston partially blocked the shot and the smoke from *Exeter* obscured the closing destroyers. The larger cruisers fought the heavy cruisers at roughly fifteen miles.

The *Houston* was so close that Evans could feel her height. Even at three-quarters of a mile, he was looking up at her guns. The smoke from the *Houston*'s guns and from the *Exeter* behind them partially clouded the enemy.

Farther west, the *Electra, Jupiter,* and *Encounter* were dealing with the four Japanese ships dispatched to sink *Exeter. Encounter,* packed with survivors from the *Kortenaer,* continued east to lay smoke for *Exeter,* and *Jupiter* did the same. The captain of HMS *Electra* had more gall. He felt his destroyer stood a chance against the four opposing ships, but it meant his demise. At under two miles, *Electra* put ten rounds into the cruiser's superstructure before the Japanese knocked out her engine. In barely a minute *Electra* was dead in the water. It was now 1728.

The cruiser, unconcerned, moved into the smoke left by the *Exeter,* leaving a single Japanese destroyer the job of finishing *Electra.* The *Jupiter* and *Encounter* were on the other side of that smoke, waiting to attack the remaining three Japanese pursuers.

The fires on *Exeter* had gotten worse and visibility was bad, so the British tin cans had an advantage. Soon the two Royal Navy destroyers were maneuvering wildly, firing at the Japanese but never from the same position, giving the impression of superiority. Such seamanship forced the Japanese to give up their bid to sink the crippled *Exeter.*

Almost three miles to the east, on the other side of the smoking *Exeter,* Evans was concerned with getting his torpedoes in the water, and he could not keep up with the events west of him.

Shells landed near him during the entire retreat, causing water to douse his deck.

The guns of the *Houston* were the only ones to keep up the entire fight. So much smoke and debris followed the shells out of her guns that they almost obscured the further ABDA column's movement. Behind the *Houston*, Evans's gunners were standing at their guns, waiting. The *Alden* remained on the disengaged side of the force as it retreated to the southeast, toward Surabaya, until Admiral Doorman ordered the American destroyers to make a torpedo attack at 1816. Now they would fall behind the cruisers and prepare to launch their fish.

In all likelihood, Evans bolted from his position on the bridge and flew down the ladder that led to the main deck. In no time he was with his torpedomen. Evans needed to assure himself that they properly set torpedo range and depth. The two Japanese columns were roughly six miles away and the Japanese ships were mostly destroyers, so a shallower swim depth, about four feet, was prescribed.

Evans ran from the first mount, then aft to the second torpedo mount. Then, after gauging that these men were handling the preparations, he returned to the bridge. In the open air on his way back there, the concussions of the cruiser's guns were growing noticeably distant as his destroyer slowed down to put her torpedoes into the water.

The cruisers fired their heavy guns blindly through the smoke at Japanese heavy cruisers fourteen miles away. With a lower profile, Evans could see only the destroyers interposed between the heavy cruisers. They became targets for his torpedomen.

Climbing the ladder to the bridge, Evans likely looked aft at the number three gun mount positioned behind the bridge. Off to port Japanese destroyers were closing range, attempting their third torpedo attack of the afternoon, but this time the Japanese destroyers were within range. It took a pair of sailors to swivel the four-inch gun and another pair to load and fire it. Standing on the open deck, without an enclosed turret—these sailors were protected by a blast shield only—they took aim. Evans had worked his crew hard and his gunners accurately fired back.

Several hits landed above the waterline on the destroyer *Asagumo*. There was no flooding but it did help keep the Japanese at a distance. The Japanese destroyers fired their third torpedo strike and retreated before the American destroyers landed too many hits and before the Allied cruisers turned their attention from the distant heavy cruisers to them. Unable to close the distance, the Japanese destroyers fired their torpedoes from too far. Then, hoping to land a hit on the retreating destroyers, at 1822 the four American destroyers turned hard to port and then starboard, firing all torpedoes.

Evans likely had low expectations of success because the torpedoes were fired at ten thousand yards—nearly six miles—giving the Japanese plenty of time to spot them and move. It was a success. Though missing, the mere presence of their torpedoes prompted the Japanese to give up the chase. At 1834 the range opened and all shooting stopped. With the Japanese gone, the force continued east, though there was still enough ABDA strength to test the Japanese. Darkness was setting.

"No one could tell what the next move would be," the captain of the *Edsall* recalled. Aboard the *Alden*, Evans must have been fuming; he had hardly participated in this fight, it seemed. He should have been tired. He had been standing and rocking in the waves for over two hours. His adrenaline was no longer peaking but he needed to be mentally awake since his crew had a long way to go to reach safe waters.

———

At this point the wounded *Exeter* traveled back to Surabaya under the escort of the Dutch destroyer *Witte de With*. The rest of the force, four cruisers and seven destroyers, attacked again at 1840, heading back west. When Evans's commander received the blinker signal *Follow me* from Admiral Doorman, the four old four-pipers fell in behind the cruisers. For the next two hours, these ships made an elliptical path, arriving at 2100 back where they had been two hours before. Over those two hours, they had found the Japanese for a five-minute period, but neither side landed hits. Star shells were launched by both sides throughout the night and Japanese spotter planes dropped flares tied to parachutes, though despite the advantage of spotter aircraft, the Japanese ships did not close for a gunfight. Instead, they remained at a distance, ready to protect the invasion force should Admiral Doorman decide to sprint toward them again.

At 2100 the ABDA force reached a critical point. The American destroyers, low on fuel, departed for Surabaya, hoping to refuel and escape for the Indian Ocean and then the west coast of Australia. However, the remaining cruisers, as well as three Dutch and British destroyers, broke off again, aimed at hugging the northern coast of Java, sneaking past the covering force, and sinking the eastern invasion force. Evans wanted to stay in the fight but his responsibility was to his own men. The *Alden* was going to attempt to reach safer waters.

It was lucky that they did. Over the next forty-eight hours, these remaining ABDA ships would be faced with a series of unfortunate events. At 2125 on the night of the twenty-seventh, the destroyer *Jupiter* exploded and sank. The column had wandered too close to the Java shoreline, and it could not be determined whether her sinking was the result of a Dutch mine or a Japanese submarine. The British destroyer *Encounter* remained on site to pick up the survivors, then turned north to join the four remaining ABDA cruisers and the Dutch destroyer *Evertsen*. Then the cruisers *Java* and *De Ruyter* were critically damaged and sank just before midnight when the force again encountered the heavy cruisers *Nachi* and *Haguro*.

Two days later, on March 1, the cruisers USS *Houston* and HMAS *Perth* and the destroyers HMS *Encounter* and HNLMS *Evertsen* were sunk when the force accidentally wandered into the landing area of Japan's western invasion force.

Evans and the American destroyer men were lucky sailors. They had avoided a terrible fate for now, but they still had to hold their breath. For the crew of the *Alden*, the sun was rapidly rising on the twenty-eighth. Japanese pilots would soon be awake and searching to destroy them. The tentacles of Japan were nearly wrapped completely around the Dutch East Indies and time was running out.

CHAPTER 5

Relegated to Escort Duty

FEBRUARY 1942–AUGUST 1943

It was quiet as a church on a Saturday night. No steeple bells rang and no choir voices drifted melodically over the water. It was a flat, calm night. But there was light.

The moon was full and there was scarcely a cloud in the sky. Keeping a watchful eye, Lieutenant Evans calmly but purposefully walked the decks of the *Alden*, stopping his sailors, inspecting their uniforms for anything that might catch the moonlight. Many were in shock after being passive observers to the winding battle just five hours before, but their cigarette habits would have to wait until daybreak. As he walked, Evans pointed out spots of the ship's structure that shone too bright, directing his sailors to paint over the places with oil. Men of a particularly pasty complexion took jobs inside the ship or used oil on themselves.

The *Alden* was soon to enter the waters of the Bali Strait, less than two miles wide at its narrowest, and there was a high chance that they could encounter patrolling Japanese destroyers. The fact that most of the ABDA force had been sunk put the Japanese at ease, but they were still hunting. Separating the islands of Java and Bali, the Bali Strait serves as a passage between the Java Sea and the Indian Ocean. It was the only way open to them for escape.

After making laps around the ship, Evans joined Commander Coley on the bridge. Lookouts' eyes were peeled, diligently searching for a torpedo track or the silhouette of an enemy ship. All they saw was the white water being displaced ahead of them by the screws of the destroyer *John D. Edwards*. As a precaution, the *John D. Ford* and *Paul Jones* were ordered to start thirty minutes after. Evans was with this first group. Perhaps this meant that they were bait for the Japanese, or perhaps being first gave them the opportunity to sneak past a distracted sentry. The plan was to hug the eastern coastline of Java and remain as far away from enemy-held Bali as possible. Evans was useful on the bridge; years earlier, as a pilot's navigator, he had been trained to recognize the profiles of Japanese ships quickly.

Coley checked the charts every few seconds and compared them to the actual environment. Evans likely retired from the bridge to monitor the sonar in the combat information center (CIC), which was one level below. The green fluorescence of the circling strobe lit up that compartment. It was probable that submarines were near, but in the shoals the biggest threat to the *Alden* came from accidentally running aground, given that the Navy had kept poor charts prior to World War II. The goal now was survival, plain and simple, but their charts of this strait might prove unreliable. Instead, they used their sonar to return readings of the depth and bearing of undersea obstacles.

At about 0130 the two destroyers reached the bottleneck that opened up into the Indian Ocean. The moon was positioned so that the Balinese landscape cast a long shadow over the expanse of ocean to the island's south. The shadow did not extend across the strait. It concealed only a portion of the water.

Minutes felt like hours until, at 0210, a lookout on the *Alden* reported a Japanese ship resting in the shadow of Bali eight thousand yards off their port bow. Runners quietly alerted the CIC, and Evans and the rest braced for impact, some men putting chins to chest while others simply stood around. Seconds went by, but no muzzle flash or thunderous boom broke the night. Evans was helpless. The four miles between them and the destroyer were enough to conceal their identity, but the illusion couldn't hold.

There was no movement. Evans had instructed his chiefs to restrict motion, noise, and light. Suspended between heaven and hell, the *Alden* carefully headed southeast toward freedom but also toward the Japanese. The Japanese destroyer was standing off to the east of the exit, and the *Alden*'s path would run parallel to its line of sight for another five miles until they could cut directly south away from the strait.

Range dropped to three miles. Then, at 0232, the suspense was shattered when the Japanese destroyer opened fire, sending overhead shells that landed a hundred yards off of the *Alden*'s disengaged side. The gunners of the *Alden* reflexively returned fire, not appreciating that Evans's blackout order extended to them. In the CIC, Evans felt even more helpless. On deck a few of his trusted sailors likely tackled these gunners, tearing them away from the triggers. They needed to remain in total darkness, and their muzzle flash would give them away.

Minutes later, at 0234, two more destroyers emerged from the shadows. There were now three destroyers in pursuit. Men screamed over one another, giving orders to shoot, then countermanding them.

The sounds of shells zooming overhead frayed many of the sailors' nerves. Columns were sent up a couple hundred yards beyond the *Alden*, and several of the misses came within twenty feet of the bridge. Then, at 0237, the three Japanese destroyers ceased fire, under orders to guard the strait should any larger force attempt to sneak through. The relief on the *Alden* was great, but Evans was not yet out of danger. Over the next couple of days, the crew slept lightly or not at all in fear of a submarine sinking them in their sleep on the way to Australia.

———

Evans and the *Alden* arrived at Exmouth Gulf on March 4. Upon arriving, the crew of the two American destroyers sighted the brand-new cruiser USS *Phoenix*, her fifteen six-inch guns glinting in the sun. She lay, unscratched, at anchor.

Astonishment quickly turned to anger. Many veterans of the Asiatic campaign felt they had been left high and dry, and while ashore, they wondered what the outcome could have been had they been better supported. Then they were tempered by a new perspective.

Several hours after the *Alden* dropped anchor, the USS *Whipple* arrived with 232 survivors of the sea tender USS *Langley* and the destroyer USS *Pope*. The *Langley*, carrying thirty-two aircraft, had been sunk in the Indian Ocean less than a week before. After this it was no struggle for the *Alden* sailors to understand their luck. To have escaped the Java Sea had been a blessing; to be in Australia now was a miracle.

Ten days after arriving at Exmouth Gulf, Evans was given command of the *Alden*. The crew had come to know him over the past eight months, and his promotion to their captain was well received. For a short time it seemed they would be sent back into action. Japanese aircraft carriers were operating unobstructed in the Indian Ocean, and many feared an air attack. Evans was personally and emotionally prepared to avenge the destruction of the ABDA fleet single-handedly, though Lieutenant Evans, as captain of the *Alden*, was not ordered back out.

His first cruise as captain was to Sydney in April 1942, the first step to returning home. Here, news of the Doolittle bombing raid on Tokyo did plenty to boost morale. At Sydney, Evans's novel status as a destroyer captain gave him access to his superiors that he'd never had before. At bars throughout Sydney, Evans would have rarely paid his own tab. Stories of his combat leadership were sought after, and Evans, always good for conversation, would have enjoyed entertaining superior officers and interested citizens in exchange for his bill.

On May 2, Evans received orders to sail to the island chain known as Vanuatu, about sixteen hundred miles northeast of Sydney. Here, Evans worked closely with the New Zealand navy in landing a battalion of engineers on the archipelago's northern island, Espiritu Santo. These engineers were tasked with constructing an airstrip that would serve as the jumping-off point for the Allies' push onto Guadalcanal three months later. Evans performed submarine protection for this convoy before setting off for Samoa.

Evans arrived at Pearl Harbor on June 7—the very time of the conclusion of the Battle of Midway, in which Japan was handed its first crushing defeat—and in two days, his ship and crew were assigned to the Navy's support fleet, delegated to escort duty and tasked with carrying supplies to and from the American West Coast. It was June 18, 1942, and the red-orange sun had just set when Evans noticed the Golden Gate on the horizon. With pride in his heart, Evans brought his destroyer gently to rest at Mare Island. He had returned home from a war zone as the captain of a bloodied destroyer, with a submarine prize and several war stories.

As much of his crew was gathered on deck as could fit. Hollers and cheers went up from all hands. Evans took pleasure in watching his crew embrace. They now had the promise of a future—for the time being at least. After living with the potential of sudden death for months, they were now home and ready to reconnect with lives that had been put on hold.

When Evans saw the fresh boots at the Mare Island Navy Yard, and the war bond and draft posters plastered around the city, it was clear to him that his oath was far from fulfilled. He looked for a captain to whom he could appeal to for a change in orders, the greenhorns awaiting assignment at Mare Island looking on with confusion when he walked by. He returned the awkward salutes he got from new reserve officers, trained in ninety days, and felt pride for their bravery. Those boys—these ninety-day wonders— had no idea what they were getting into. If he could, he wanted to be beside them, immediately back in the fight.

As a destroyer captain, Evans had done and would do his damn best, though his next battle would not come immediately. He would not detach from the *Alden*, and since she was an old ship, she would not be sent in with the new vessels that were being minted in shipyards in Houston, Texas, and Tacoma, Washington, each day. The *Alden*'s crew, some of the only experienced sailors in the nation, would be kept on fleet logistics until further notice.

While swallowing this fact, Evans went to the work needed to prepare the *Alden* for a stay at Mare Island. The engineers, mechanics, sonarmen, and gunners all had lists of the supplies they needed to refresh their equipment. The men who would clean the latrines had already pulled the short straws, and the rest worked to clean their general areas. Ammunition was brought from belowdecks and stored in a brick bunker on the island. Then there was a short ceremony.

Evans was presented with a pair of golden oak leaves, signifying that he was a lieutenant commander, and a Bronze Star for his actions against the Japanese submarine on January 20. Then Evans was handed staff chores. Many of his men submitted requests for ship or service transfer, and Evans wanted to see several of them promoted or trained in new skills. Some even received his commendations for medals or promotions. After several days, Evans was excused of his responsibilities and at last traveled from San Francisco to see his family at their home in Long Beach.

Margaret had been living with the stress of her husband's possible death for nearly five months. The American press had done well to sugarcoat the early events of the war, though her worst fears were vindicated by the widely covered fall of Singapore. Since his departure from American soil, his sons, Ernest and David, had grown two years older and were now ten and nine, respectively. As they ascended in school, they clung to memories of their father as a tugboat captain in San Francisco. They could not comprehend the magnitude of his newest responsibilities.

He did not talk about his experiences. One day, though, his children would hear of the ghosts from the Java Sea that haunted him. He likely chose to tell stories of the wonderful places he had seen. At night Ernest Jr. would sit with his father while he read. Evans often read of Navy battles and Navy matters, making an impression on his older boy.

During the day, Evans decked himself out in his dress whites for his wife, proudly presenting his new lieutenant commander's epaulets. That after ten years he still had Margaret on his arm was no small source of pride. For his children it was good to see their parents happy and together for the first time in two years. Soon, though, the wounds of his absences were opened again.

Evans had twelve days with his family before reporting back to the *Alden*. He would get his fight, but not before the *Alden*'s utility was exhausted and a new command was available to him. So, over the coming months, Evans kept an eye on newspapers from Seattle and Houston, the locations of the two shipyards with the responsibility of building destroyers, one of which he would take back to the Pacific to resume the fight. In the meantime, he fulfilled his responsibilities to fleet logistics and returned to the *Alden*.

She never again sailed into certain danger, but danger would not disappear entirely. American shipping was under the very real threat of Japanese and German submarine attack, and Evans would give his best to keep the supply arteries flowing, his decrepit old four-piper shuttling convoys of matériel and personnel between California and Hawaii.

Over the next eight months, Evans made the round trip nine times. For a lethargic supply convoy, it is an eight- to eleven-day cruise, about thirty-six hundred miles. In his ship's log, Evans wrote the same daily: "steaming as before, acting as anti-submarine screen for convoy." Evans chose a different route each time to avoid a pattern of movement. At Pearl Harbor and San Francisco, Evans learned details of naval battles as they leaked.

At the end of March 1943, Evans departed the Pacific for the warmer Caribbean.

After transiting the Panama Canal, he turned his destroyer south toward the naval base at Trinidad and was greeted by weather before reaching his destination. Walls of water slammed into the ship, shattering the double-paned glass windows of the bridge as Evans stood shoulder to shoulder with his helmsman and directed him to steer into the forty-foot waves. Down below, the crew sat on the deck in life vests as they rolled as much as fifty-eight degrees in the swell. The storm passed without damage, and soon this was another memory at sea. Another feat to tell about in the future.

In May, Evans visited Haiti, Puerto Rico, and Cuba and escorted merchant ships before his tenure aboard the *Alden* ended. After arriving at the Brooklyn Naval Yard on June 2, Evans handed over command to a Marine second lieutenant for a period of maintenance. While waiting at the train station in New York, Evans sought out a newspaper.

He returned home the first week of July 1943 and again spent time at his home in Long Beach. Evans's older son recalled to a journalist in the 1970s that his father had been busy reading at nights during his time home. He enjoyed mysteries, and after his experiences in the Java Sea, he continued to bore into naval strategy and tactics. In reading the great sea battles between Britain and Germany of the previous world war, Evans Sr. considered the merit of steering into the previous shell splash under the presumption that the enemy would correct their aim.

At the end of August, Evans made travel arrangements to go to the Seattle–Tacoma shipyard. His orders were to report to a new *Fletcher*-class destroyer. It would soon be commissioned, and Evans was to report early with a handful of officers. By August 1943, 101 of these destroyers had been put into service. A whole new fleet had been born, though old hands would sail them into battle.

CHAPTER 6

"I Intend to Go in Harm's Way"

AUGUST 1943–JANUARY 1944

On reporting to Seattle–Tacoma, Evans was brought to the ship by jeep for a tour. The shipyard was a cacophony of noise, for nearly half a dozen other vessels were being built within earshot, and the maelstrom of sound was violent: Contractors were welding flat steel plates to gun mounts; rivets were being driven home into their prepared holes. Amid the hive of work, radiant sparks and pungent hydrogen fluoride gas harassed Evans's senses as he stepped from the jeep and walked toward his new command.

She was an attractive ship. The five gun turrets—two forward and two aft, super-firing one gun above another, and the fifth turret aft of the second funnel—were her main battery. The two quintuple torpedo tubes—one just forward of the third five-inch gun and the other between her two stacks—were also powerful features. She was, foremost, a submarine hunter and aircraft killer. DD-557 had a clean profile, showing no sign of unnecessary accoutrements. There were more improvements to her than met the casual eye. She was a *Fletcher*-class destroyer, the Navy's work-horse design. Christened the United States Ship *Johnston* at her launch the previous March, she had been named for Lieutenant John V. Johnston of the Union Navy in the Civil War.

Three hundred seventy-six feet long and nearly forty feet in the beam, she drew nearly eighteen feet of water and displaced more than twenty-five hundred tons full load—a full third heavier than pre-*Fletcher* destroyers. After building more than a hundred of them, the Navy had seen the need for key redesigning, and *Johnston* was one of the first of the new *Fletchers*. Experience had shown them to be top-heavy, so topside armor was thinned, and the after superstructure lowered by a deck. Evans arrived in time to oversee the installation of the sonar gear and fearsome antiaircraft capability: ten Bofors 40mm guns in five motorized twin turrets and seven Oerlikon 20mm cannons.

She was every inch a fighting ship, as yet unbloodied, but Evans had every intention—he was eager—to take her into battle.

Inside, one of the first things that Evans noticed was the sound. He knew the hollow, dull, muffled echo of outside noise that worked through the heavier hide of the battleship *Colorado* and the cruiser *Pensacola*, but inside the lightly armored DD-557, sounds carried unmistakably, right down to workers outside belching.

After viewing the bridge and his sea cabin on the top deck, he moved down, eventually five levels below to the berth deck, which housed the enlisted crew. Evans was trailed by a mix of shipyard employees and sailors. As they walked, he began to assimilate the routes he would take between his stations. His leather captain's chair at the front-right corner of the bridge was clearly a spot where his crew would come to find him. Visibility from here was improved in the new *Fletchers* by the addition of open platforms on the bridge wings. Behind his chair the ladder just outside the bridge would deposit him by his sea cabin two decks down.

Above the bridge was the largest improvement Evans found with this new class of destroyer: a new Mark 37 gun director sitting just above the bridge. From this armored box, five men would coordinate gunfire in battle aided by a highly advanced fire control radar on the roof; the radar would take gunlaying out of their hands and keep the guns trained on targets, even account for the ship's maneuvering. The technology on the *Fletchers* was new. Evans was not entirely up-to-date, but he knew enough about sonar and electrical engineering to oversee the radarmen who would arrive from training in New York and Northern California.

In general, all the essential spaces were larger than in the earlier destroyers. The combat information center, radio room, and officers' wardroom could accommodate more men. Evans took note that the extra space in the wardroom would accommodate his surgeon, who would operate there during battle. In the mess more men could be fed despite the eighteen bunks that were chained to the wall to support overflow crew.

Everywhere, the ship was pristine—no corrosion from months of salt water. Paint was smooth, not cracked; watertight doors were not rusted; and miles of electrical lines were fastened and woven carefully through the bulkheads, nothing yet frayed or torn, so there was no risk of an electrical fire.

Evans came prepared for his crew to be green and from different backgrounds. The kids in technical positions were liable not to mix well with the boys from Alabama and Memphis who would be manning the ammunition hoists. The college boys assigned to his radar and sonar equipment might not know the value of scraping paint, but they would come right as long as they followed his orders and kept themselves out of the chief's quarters. No matter the war, disrupting that sanctuary of knowledge and experience was a sin greater even than not knowing how to swim—a charge of which many of his new sailors would be guilty.

———

The crew was not needed aboard until shortly before her commissioning. After boot camp and extended training, hundreds would pile into trains for the journey to the West Coast. After his initial tour, Evans was told where he could find the early arrivals. Among the first men Evans met was his gunnery officer, Lieutenant Robert Hagen.

Upon meeting, the two sized each other up and determined that they made a good pair. They both were serious but had a sense of humor. After Pearl Harbor, Hagen had left the University of Texas after his first semester to enroll in a ninety-day reserve officer training program, and he had then been made assistant communications officer aboard the destroyer *Aaron Ward*, which had been headed for Guadalcanal. Hagen had Evans's complete attention as he related his experiences on that ship.

In the waters off Guadalcanal, Hagen had been wounded during a vicious night battle. About that, he said, "I didn't consider myself lucky at the time the doctors were cutting a useless artery from my arm and removing shell fragments from my leg, but those wounds kept me off the *Aaron Ward* when she went down later off Tulagi." After that experience, Hagen had decided on a rating change, reasoning that in communications one mistake meant punishment, but in gunnery one hit made a hero.

From his arrival on August 9 through the end of the month, Evans worked to familiarize himself with the ship. He labored to understand the systems and their backups, and he seared into his mind all protocols and contingencies to follow in the case of battle damage. Evans learned alongside his men, who continued to trickle in. By the end of August, a skeleton crew was ready for a trial at sea.

The "Fast Cruise / Sea Trial" phase marks that point of a ship's life when the basic systems—boilers, firerooms, propellers, and anchor machinery—are tested. From September through early October, Evans steamed his ship around Washington's coast. DD-557 finally raised her commission pennant on October 27, 1943, at 1059, when Evans's USS *Johnston* joined the fleet. She was placed in commission by Captain H. K. Stubbs, the supervisor of the Seattle–Tacoma shipyard. After reading from a script at the ceremony, Captain Stubbs stood back and gave Evans the deck. With a full heart, Evans stepped forward, cleared his throat, and began. He read from a letter endorsed by the Navy secretary. It was vague but covered their orders. Then, at 1103, Evans folded the letter and put it in his pocket, observing the formation around him as he did.

His crew was standing on the fantail of the ship, lined up before him. To them Evans declared, "This is going to be a fighting ship. I intend to go in harm's way and anyone who doesn't want to go along had better get off right now." The green sailors just stared back at him. In front of them was a calm, composed destroyer captain. Evans, perhaps sensing some skepticism, reinforced upon them his determination to fight. He explained his experiences in the Battle of the Java Sea, and his words were clear. He would not hesitate to put them all in the line of fire.

At 1115 Evans finished speaking, turned to his left, and shook Captain Stubbs's hand. Standing behind Evans was his executive officer, Lieutenant Commander Howard Baker. Evans turned to Baker and gave the order to prepare the ship for departure.

The *Johnston* left dock at 1215 and anchored at Puget Sound by 1400. Throughout that afternoon men got acquainted with their berths, which on the *Johnston* were bunks stacked three high. Before commissioning, Evans's personal effects had been brought aboard, so he had the evening to himself before calling his officers and chiefs to meet in the wardroom. Evans heard Brooklyn accents mix with Jersey, and Midwestern with Southern. While he set himself up in his private cabin, he listened to the life that was being breathed into his vessel.

Each enlisted man was provided Navy regulation thirteen square feet for sleeping accommodations. One sailor with terrible hygiene could ruin everything. Before the end of a shakedown cruise, the light sleepers and weak stomachs were found and moved toward the stability of the keel. The heavy sleepers took the liability of being placed near the hull, betting that the roll of the ship would not wake them. The eighteen men whose berths were in the mess hall were voluntarily the first awake; they ate breakfast next to their folded-up bunks.

———

Even in wartime, the commissioning of a new ship was allowed to be celebrated. Some of Evans's young crew might have fancied themselves salty senior chiefs already, but Evans knew all too well how green they were. No sailors could be truly Navy until they had pulled three consecutive nights on watch, gotten chewed out by a senior, missed a family gathering, or cursed the day they chose the Navy over the Army. But that night his sailors donned their best for a formal commissioning ball, with wives and girlfriends invited to a hotel in Seattle where sponsors had rented out the ballroom.

After the bar was drunk dry, the ship's doctor mixed a punch he called a "pink lady," spiked with 180-proof grain alcohol. The powerful spirits proved too much for many of the recruits. Almost Evans's entire crew was teenagers who not only had never been to sea, but a significant portion had never drunk to excess. This evening it showed. The ball became a commissioning brawl as intercity rivalries surfaced, and many men took to fistfights.

Famously, Lieutenant (jg) Ellsworth Welch—another reservist officer—arrived with his future wife on his arm just as furniture began to fly. The scene was not the formal event that Welch had promised his fiancée. In Bob Hagen's words, "it was stupendous." Years later Hagen recalled that his jaw was nearly broken when the wife of one of the enlisted sailors hit him across the face with her purse.

Evans knew to maintain a degree of separation. Well practiced in restraint, he watched from the side, happy to sip on brandy if only when he felt the need to hide his grin. Eventually the shore patrol arrived and broke up the fighting, though the military police realized the importance of the evening, and nobody was arrested. This night, all across Seattle, a new holiday—Navy Day—was being celebrated, in recognition of the fact that in the coming weeks thousands of sailors would put to sea, many never to return.

After speaking with the military police and seeing that the evening had not gotten out of hand, Evans left for his cabin. When he descended the stairs in the morning, he greeted Hagen at the breakfast table with a half smile as he muttered, "Great party," and slid across the table a bill for ten thousand dollars.

———

At Puget Sound the *Johnston* went through her fitting out, taking aboard ammunition—five-inch rounds, armor-piercing for surface combat and bombarding shore fortifications, antipersonnel for invasion support; proximity-fused antiaircraft shells; and phosphorous star shells for night illumination. Then there were torpedoes, depth charges, and various types of antiaircraft ammunition, as well as food, medical supplies, and spare parts—all had to be documented and properly stored.

Ernest Evans lost no time in winning the respect of his crew. He knew he had impressed them at the commissioning ball by making light conversation with some of their girlfriends and wives. The men knew they liked their captain's gift of gab, but more to the point, his ease with the women gave them reassurance that their young men would be well looked after. They would receive less grief or worry in letters home. As his crew clambered aboard the day after the party, Evans could hear apprehension, excitement, frustration, fear, curiosity, and optimism in their voices, but he had already taken the first steps to presenting himself as the strong commanding figure aboard.

From October 28 to November 10, the *Johnston* and her crew remained loading supplies at Puget Sound, and Margaret drove up from Los Angeles with Ernest Jr. and David to be with her husband. Evans delegated duties to his executive officer and spent time with his family.

Evans tried not to take himself too seriously; he was just a good father. His whole childhood had been focused on leaving Oklahoma behind, and now he wanted his boys to be able to expect more from their home than he'd had, but still they needed to work hard and make something of themselves. He taught as many lessons as he could in their time together. He could not promise that he would be home soon, and it was difficult to look at his boys and know how much they would miss him. But it was inevitable and had to be accepted—another lesson that had to be learned. The family returned to Long Beach, and the *Johnston* began her sea trials.

From November 11 to 14, she operated just off the Washington coastline, testing her vital systems. Then, on the fifteenth, she turned south for San Diego. After three days of plowing through the Pacific seaway, many became ill. Those who were seasick ate sparingly, preferring to avoid the trip from the mess hall to the stern to vomit. Evans laughed. He did not grow ill or stumble as he walked about. He had long ago acquired his sea legs, so he enjoyed his food. The cooks—mostly Filipino or Black—aboard the *Johnston* particularly liked him because he treated them equally. In a still segregated Navy, the cooks lived apart from the rest. Evans, who could recall the treatment of American Indians in the white world, knew that such segregation was ignorant.

The *Johnston* arrived in San Diego but left a day later, putting out to sea for twelve days of uninterrupted practice, with a plan to arrive back at Seattle by the thirtieth of December. The intensity of training forced the crew to realize that they needed to work together. Once the crew accepted that, they saw Evans as even more of a leadership figure, and made attempts to figure him out. They knew of his nickname, "Big Chief," and doubtless wondered what part being Cherokee played in his psyche. Eventually, though, they just accepted him as an enigma.

It was not that Evans knew more than anybody else; he simply knew how to get along. High school and certainly the Naval Academy had taught him to work on a team, and he had learned how to make his home wherever he went. The young sailors in his care did not understand that yet. Evans's power aboard ship was virtually absolute, but he was not an authoritarian. He was humble and even derived a degree of amusement from his power. He did not allow his authority to separate him from his crew, but if needed, he could enforce his will.

He led his officers in a cryptic and light-handed manner and would give them responsibilities sometimes without ever saying a word, just to test how they could manage. He worked to defy labeling. It appears that Evans was aware of the widespread belief in the Navy that a captain could be understood by where he sat at mealtime and that Satan sat at the head of the table. Evans changed where he sat.

Evans's critics were few and far between, it seemed. He was thought of as a man of indomitable will. He accomplished whatever he sought to achieve, whether it be earning a Naval Academy appointment or embedding a concrete bunker into a cliffside. Evans had a way of approaching tasks from a different point of view, which enabled him to achieve results others could not attain and succeed where other captains often failed. He bound his crew together months before they reached the combat theater and achieved unit cohesion rare for just a few weeks at sea. The men had many occasions to bond.

Evans was an advocate for the little guy. He maintained that some wrongdoing could be overlooked if the sailors worked hard. One particular sailor had brought aboard a case of beer while at San Diego, which this sailor drank in one night during the twelve-day sea trial. Once that sailor had been caught, Bob Hagen began to tear into him with the full power of his lungs. Hagen then restricted the sailor to the brig to sober up. Evans was aware of the rumblings aboard—his crew wondered what their skipper would do in a situation without a clear answer—so he used the attention to let his crew get to know him. The next day at captain's mast, Evans ordered Hagen to advocate in the sailor's defense.

It became a notable part of the ship's lore, and it was a sight to see Hagen provide his tongue-in-cheek defense, but Evans's motivation was deeper. They were sailing into a war zone, and Evans needed to keep the atmosphere light. His men were adjusting to life in the Navy while simultaneously preparing for war. The fact that Hagen—a famous hardnose—took the joke was a testament to his understanding of his captain as a nuanced leader of men. Hagen, despite his youth, also had experience sending men into danger. Indeed, Hagen reminded Evans often of his first posting in the Navy.

Before reporting to the *Aaron Ward*, Hagen had been assigned to a recruiting station in the Midwest. Here the five Sullivan brothers from Waterloo, Iowa, had walked into his office, desiring to serve together on the same ship. After receiving the go-ahead from his boss, Hagen allowed it. All five brothers died in November 1942 when the cruiser USS *Juneau* was torpedoed the morning after a night battle left her crippled. Almost every sailor aboard the *Johnston* knew this story and probably thought about it as they exercised off the West Coast of the United States.

The *Johnston* did reach Seattle by December 30 and remained anchored there into the New Year. Then she steamed for San Diego on January 2. There they practiced submarine depth charge drills with a live submarine, honing the sonarmen's skills and preparing the crew for the radical turns of this type of combat. When a submarine was not present for training, Evans had to make do with his imagination.

Evans spent a majority of his time making torpedo runs on phantom battleships. Standing nearest the helmsman, giving course changes for a smooth attack, Evans readied his crew for the battle when their ten explosive-tipped fish would race toward a Japanese warship. "We thought maybe he was a little torpedo-happy," recalled Bill Mercer, one of the younger sailors on the ship, but Evans's lighter weapons got a chance to practice, too. Evans was almost paternal in the way that he instilled in his men his passion for preparedness.

Aircraft towing target sleeves flew overhead one afternoon. Hundreds of tracer bullets filled the air, their paths illuminated by a combination of ignited magnesium and oxidized salt. These tracer bullets were set in clips and passed into the gun by hand. The action was enough to cause excited men to fumble the ammunition, and the shooting was not accurate, though fortunately for the pilot the cable towing the target sleeve was long. The result of the drill filled Evans with apprehension, but Bob Hagen— governing the target selection in the gun director—was brought to outright disgust. Hagen was glad the ship's first kill was not friendly. Hagen wrote sarcastically to a friend in Texas that he should "stay out of our gun range, anything can happen." Evans gave the *Johnston*'s no-nonsense gun boss free rein to call the crew to general quarters anytime he liked. Hagen used this authority so liberally that *Johnston* acquired a nickname long before she reached a combat zone: *GQ Johnny*.

The crew noted that Evans gave them room in the critical weeks after commissioning to make the mistakes they needed to make in order to learn. There was much to get used to. During bombardment practice at San Clemente Island, the concussion of the five-inch guns sent those on the bridge with weak legs grabbing for something steady, whereas experienced seamen would not have flinched.

The *Johnston* was reported "ready for sea" by January 10, but the next night while docked in the San Diego Navy base, Evans's men went out for a night of drinking and got into a fight with military police. The next day, rather than throw the book at the men—Evans did not want to lose his fighting sailors—he enlisted the support of one of his junior officers.

One of the brightest of Evans's crew was Lieutenant (jg) Edward DiGardi, the assistant communications officer. DiGardi had been in his second year of law school when the war began. He joined the midshipmen program at Hastings College of Law and graduated as an ensign on February 17, 1943. In a preliminary hearing to see if courts-martial were necessary, DiGardi successfully defended the men and had their charges dropped. Happy with the outcome, Evans gave DiGardi a wink and a sly grin before exiting the courtroom.

In trusting his junior officer with this proceeding, Evans won his crew a victory for morale. However, the crew was soon hit by the sudden loss of its first chief boatswain's mate, who went AWOL. Evans was days from forming with a battleship force en route to Hawaii, and the lack of an experienced enlisted man in this vital position left a wide leadership void. So Evans went ashore in search of a replacement.

He found him in Clyde Burnett, who became a man on whom Evans would rely. He had joined the service the year before the attack on Pearl Harbor and was on the island during the raid. Thereafter, he joined the submarine fleet, figuring that "being aboard a submarine was probably the quickest way to get back at the Japs." After some time, he grew tired of submarines, requested a transfer, and arrived in San Diego shortly before New Year's Day 1944. He had been awaiting reassignment when Evans walked into the personnel office and requested any available senior enlisted man.

Burnett had been lying on a cot at the receiving station before an escort took him to the personnel office. "I met with a very sharp Commander who advised me that he had a new ship with a new crew that he planned to send to the war zone very shortly and the ship was in need of a Chief Boatswain's Mate," Burnett recalled. Having not been home since 1939, Burnett was cautious, but Evans was convincing and brought him aboard.

At 1700 on the twelfth, Evans left San Diego for San Pedro with Task Unit 53.5.8, a cruiser force with a destroyer screen under the command of Captain Edward Solomons in the veteran destroyer *Morris*. While they were joining the formation, the only work that was required of the *Johnston*'s two helmsmen was to steer and request power from the engine room. To this end Evans stood directing his helmsman for the course and the lee helmsman for specific power. As the lee helmsman slowly pushed the engine control lever forward, the ship picked up speed smoothly and the helmsman moved them into position with the cruisers. Men lined the rail and climbed atop gun turrets, waving their caps as the cruisers welcomed them into their screen.

After a few hours at sea with the heavy cruisers, the *Johnston* met up with Rear Admiral Jesse Oldendorf's Task Group 53.5, and at 1500 this task group met up with the remainder of Task Force 53, under command of Rear Admiral Thomas Connolly. The Fifth Fleet, under overall command of Admiral Raymond Spruance, was the first iteration of new aircraft carriers, battleships, cruisers, transports, and destroyers that would take the fight to the Pacific.

From the bridge Evans could see the expansive fleet around him. In the wardroom with fresh charts spread out, Evans, together with his reservist officers, eyed the Philippines and the island chains that trailed them to the south. Thousands of miles of ocean lay between Evans and his men and their destination, and they knew where their attention must focus: The Marshall Islands would need to be attacked first.

This was now Evans's tenth journey to Hawaii, and since it was his crew's first, he sat and observed their behavior. It was apparent that they were heading into danger. Some men were suddenly silent, and others took to nervous conversation. Some seemed forgetful, and many could not sleep. Evans strode the ship and offered kind words when he could. As a leader he inspired great confidence in his people. "We were on a High Class ship because this Captain was High Class," recalled Lieutenant Hagen.

Once with Task Force 53, Evans's crew got an impression of the part they were to play. Seeing their position within a larger surface fleet was helpful to them. The *Johnston* was cruising on the outer edge of this attack force. This provided the antiaircraft gunners, the depth charge crews, and the main battery gunners with a sense of place. If aircraft or submarines were detected, they were the first line of defense to the cruisers, battleships, and aircraft carriers.

At times the scene was almost festive. Aircraft returning from patrols performed aileron rolls, tipping their wings to Evans and his sailors on deck. It was the first time many of his men had seen a great fleet. Sitting in his brown chair at the front-right corner of the bridge—a compartment barely one hundred square feet in size—Evans took it all in. Behind him men were gaining skill with their jobs. They asked questions and made mistakes. Evans learned the voices of those with roles of responsibility, and by the end of the first week, without turning his head, he could likely address them by name.

Most of the green crew, despite knowing the fundamentals of their jobs, still lacked an appreciation of the seriousness of the mission, and Evans confided to his journal that they needed an impression to be made. Once they were in the open sea and in the company of capital ships, the training intensified, with particular attention to the divisions that would face the most stress in combat.

He made sure his radiomen had scripts to read. He needed them to be able to communicate clearly with Marines onshore. A salvo landing off mark meant ineffective support or, worse, the casualties of friendly fire. Evans required attention to detail of his sonarmen. The pair of men sitting in this twenty-two-square-foot compartment behind the bridge was made to master the art of fixing a position with sound pulses. Fortunately, the mass of ships around them provided many objects to locate and listen for. Throughout the next few days, these sailors kept tabs on the movements of the ships around them by listening to the sound heard from the receiver underneath the ship and by watching the green strobe on the monitor in front of them.

The *Johnston* herself was one ship in a fleet strewn across the ocean like pieces on a chessboard. To Evans the scene resembled other fleet exercises, but to those of his 314-man crew who had not participated in those, the mass of ships gathered brought home the reality of war. When Task Force 53 arrived off the coast of Lahaina on January 21, 1944, Evans and his crew watched from the *Johnston* as the green hills and sandy shores grew larger. Finally, something more inspiring than the massive fleet around them captivated their attention.

From his perch Evans looked hopefully at the beaches, but this visit would be starved of shore liberty. The *Johnston*'s anchor was sent crashing down before midday and only select sailors went ashore for ammunition. Evans had responsibilities. This evening the commander of Task Unit 53.5.2 had the force's destroyer captains aboard his flagship, USS *Santa Fe*, to discuss fire support.

Evans spent the evening with captains and admirals, poring over the movements and tactics of the squadron. Big-picture conversations can divert a captain's attention from his personal responsibilities to his men, but Evans was well-grounded. After the meetings, when Evans's gig was hoisted back aboard his ship, he made his way to his cabin and certainly passed men leisurely smoking cigarettes, completely unconcerned with the content of his meeting. The trade wind that was funneled between Maui and Lanai cooled the deck, and enterprising crewmen had rigged hammocks and lay suspended, appreciating their circumstances.

Shortly after first light on the twenty-second, Evans's gig was again lowered into the ocean. His men were awake, eating and smoking at their 40mm and 20mm gun tubs after the dawn general quarters drill, and their conversations carried over the water and reached Evans until he neared the destroyer *Morris*. Aboard the *Morris* the destroyer captains discussed with the commander of Task Unit 53.5.8 the patrol schedule, what parts of the formation they would protect, and the speed, turning, and defensive limitations of the formation's largest ships.

Evans returned from this meeting to find men working hard. Enlisted leaders like Bob Hollenbaugh were holding PT drills, and sailors with technical jobs never quite rested. The gunners practiced the firing sequences in their bunks, the lookouts studied ship profiles on their downtime, and the radiomen practiced drafting messages in Morse code should their equipment fail.

Evans must have been pleased that the crew knew he expected them to perform. Lieutenant Welch recalled that Evans "never quite had to spell out the consequences; the very thought that the skipper might become disappointed was enough." Upon reaching Hawaii, the crew felt that Evans's expectations of them had grown considerably, and they labored to keep up. With battle looming, it was good that Evans's leadership style tended toward strictness. He did not often vocalize his intent, which likely allowed his crew to build up their confidence; instead he relied on his junior officers to exercise his will. Evidently, Evans's tactics achieved his goal of having a proficient crew. The *Johnston* was requested to leave for the war zone before the second day of meetings ended, and a day later he committed to his journal that "it is surprising how fast the crew has shaken down."

The waters off Maui were busy on the afternoon of the twenty-second as the *Johnston's* anchor came rattling aboard. Under Rear Admiral Thomas Connolly, Task Force 53's destination was the Kwajalein Atoll, one of twenty-nine rings of islands that form the Marshall Islands group. These rings are visible portions of underwater volcanoes, and some are eighty miles end to end. The Japanese used the expansive lagoons to protect their ships from wild seas and enemy attacks.

In the late thirties and early forties, Japan placed artillery pieces on the islands that were large enough to support them. The Navy was going to attack only the atolls whose islands had runways built on them or whose interior lagoons were large enough to house a fleet. Kwajalein Atoll met both criteria.

Though "much anxiety reigns," Evans wrote, "the crew is conscious of the importance of this operation." Their incessant training seemed to emphasize the danger of the job they were going to do. Kwajalein Atoll lay more than twenty-six hundred miles west–southwest of Hawaii, halfway to Australia. Zigzagging to avoid detection, the fleet would reach Kwajalein in under eight days. It would be less than three months after their commissioning party in Seattle that Evans and his crew would finally enter the war zone. There they would be tasked with bombarding enemy-held islands, scanning Neptune's ocean for submarines, and, if called upon, releasing torpedoes at enemy warships.

On the way, gun captains drew the majority of Evans's attention, and his torpedo crews became accustomed to what was a loose friendship with their captain. His sonarmen likely got to know him at odd hours of the night as he visited the bridge. Evans was a personal leader, earning that praise for being "high class" and a good man. "Never in my life have I met a man like Commander Evans," recalled a sailor of his. None of the commentary had anything to say about him being disagreeable. Evans was labeled "torpedo-happy" by Bill Mercer and considered by some to be too aggressive, but as his crew sailed into battle, they all respected their captain. Everyone from the machinist mates to the sonarmen wanted to earn his respect in return. As the *Johnston* headed toward Kwajalein, the sonarmen felt the most pressure. The Japanese submarine force was strong and fully intended to make the American Navy pay for every mile it drew closer to Tokyo, and all their eyes were on the Fifth Fleet.

On the twenty-fifth, Evans refueled from a tanker. He ordered the lee helmsman to match speed; then oil lines were quickly tossed over, along with a pulley system. While the ship was fueling, newspapers were sent over. Evans watched from the open bridge as sailors picked the first papers from the bag. They all thumped their chests a little that evening when "we noted the 'Press News' from the United States [was] heralding our invasion of the Marshalls," Evans wrote.

The staging areas off Kwajalein Atoll were still a couple days away as Evans and his officers read the papers in the wardroom. At Kwajalein Atoll, the *Johnston* would meet up with a tractor group that would land Marines on their first target. As the evening of the twenty-fifth faded away, Evans learned from enlisted leaders that fear of Japanese submarines was spreading belowdecks. It was justified, too. On the twenty-sixth, a contact report from the sonar crew brought Evans from his sea cabin at the shrieking sound of the Klaxon. Within less than one minute, everybody was at battle stations.

Evans entered the bridge, got on the public address system, and declared the contact. The talker was standing next to him, waiting to give word to the depth charge handlers to release their explosives. Evans was prepared to give the word as soon as sonarmen reported the sounds of a propeller in the water. Several tense minutes passed but no further contacts were reported. Once heartbeats returned to normal, calmer minds guessed that a large school of fish had broken up after the *Johnston* passed. Evans quickly returned to the public address system and explained his thoughts to the crew.

There was reassurance in this false alarm. If his crew had not been honed to fear their unseen enemy, then their response would have been slovenly. They were not a battle-tested crew yet, but they were getting there, and the coming invasion of the Marshalls would provide the opportunity to grow. Every mile southwest increased the possibility of running into a Japanese sub, though by the predawn hours of January 31 no attack had occurred. At 0130 that day, the *Johnston* left Task Force 53 and headed with Task Unit 53.5.2 to her fire support zone off Roi and Mellu Islands of the Kwajalein Atoll. At 0233 the *Johnston* left the heavy cruisers of that Task Unit to stand alone in her fire support position. The moon was bright, almost the same conditions that had cast shadows over the sea the night Evans had left the Java Sea via the Bali Strait twenty-three months before.

CHAPTER 7

Island-Hopping

FEBRUARY 1944–JULY 1944

Shortly after midnight on the thirty-first, Evans brought his destroyer due west to a rally point off Mellu Island. Southwest of the larger Roi Island—the most northern in the atoll—Mellu was attacked first because there was a deep-water channel that would immediately allow passage into the lagoon within the atoll once Mellu was captured. From air reports, Evans knew that Mellu was home to several pillboxes and a light garrison of Japanese soldiers. Evans had been sweating over maps of the atoll for days and understood that those islands guarding the entrances to the atoll would be attacked first. In the grid of ocean off Mellu/Roi, Evans was supposed to meet a group of Marine-laden Landing Ship Tanks (or LSTs).

The crew knew the game was on when they left behind the force of cruisers at 0233. Immediately, lookouts became more alert. The crew was apprehensive and tense as a tuning fork as they anticipated their first combat operation.

Evans was a pragmatic leader who had been in combat before. He knew his men could not be expected to be without doubts, but he would have expected them to perform their jobs to the best of their abilities. As the moon moved in the sky, Evans's lookouts kept their eyes peeled, straining to find this LST group among the black waves and breaking whitecaps. Evans strode the bridge behind them, using his calm and reassuring presence as a tether. At 0248 his lookouts related to him the sighting of LSTs. However, despite the skill of these navigators in arriving there from across the globe, Evans recognized a misstep. The LST group was farther east than planned.

Evans took note of his closeness to Roi Island, then turned to the LST group bobbing in the waves off to starboard. The plan called for a couple extra miles separating his destroyer from Roi's west coast, which reports confirmed held artillery; however, the LSTs could not perform that coordinated movement in the dark. Throughout the night, Evans's lookouts watched Roi with suspicion. Certainly, Evans was aware that this was not the last time he would be expected to perform more than had been tasked to him.

Lights were dimmed and the bridge was silent. Evans at some point likely retreated to his private cabin belowdecks. The sea cabin behind the bridge would have him on the bridge quickly in case of a fight, but the breeze that blew over the deck level was superior for sleep, and the porthole of his private cabin would let the draft in.

Off his starboard beam, the LSTs rocked in the waves. Through his porthole Evans could have occasionally heard the voices of Marines echo over the water. Beyond them, only two miles away and clearly visible in the moonlight, was Roi Island. The *Johnston* was backlit to the defenders on Roi, but the artillery remained silent through the night.

When the sun rose on January 31, Evans's world changed. At 0652 when he barked, "Open fire!" he was no longer the captain of an unbloodied destroyer. The *Johnston* threw out two hundred main-caliber shells in ninety minutes, reducing two fortified artillery installations.

Next, the 40mm crews cut loose and in half an hour fired seven hundred rounds. Japanese soldiers running between cover were cut down. The island was barely large enough to offer cover. Very quickly the Japanese had no place to hide, so they dug into the sand. They responded mostly with rifle fire, though a few rushed shots from artillery pieces sent columns of water rising a hundred yards from the *Johnston*.

Evans was like a Norseman pacing behind a shield wall of his countrymen, and his loud commands steadied his sailors. At 0845 Evans ceased fire and began to move his ship off the coast to screen for submarines. However, dozens of LSTs filled the sea near and around him, and he could not maneuver until they turned toward the beach.

Temporarily without jobs, sailors came topside to wait and watch the scene play out.

The smells of salt water and burning diesel fuel were better than the sweat and odor belowdecks, Evans well knew. The view was better, too, though Evans had to remind his officers to deal quickly with any who thought it wise to stand in the open and gawk. When the LSTs suddenly lurched forward, they set the crew buzzing; crouched behind quarter-inch blast shields, they realized that now at last the war was real.

After the LSTs cleared, Evans took his ship and spent the afternoon screening a fire support unit farther out to sea. Belowdecks, men were served food. That morning the crew in the handling room had worked up an appetite loading shell after shell onto the hoists that fed the five-inch guns. Bob Hagen had picked his strongest men to work in the handling room; the work to haul the thirty-pound shells was exhausting, and they ate ravenously. After this action Hagen had to say, "I knew, after that show, that we had a good ship and a Captain who could strike fighting spirit from his men the way steel strikes spark from flint."

The night came and the crew slept unbothered by work, except occasional gunfire and rising star shells in the distance. The men needed rest. With more tankers and transports arriving and additional warships to follow, Evans's superiors were on a tight timetable to help secure the atoll and its vital anchorage. Mellu was just the first step. Orders came the next morning to seize Namur Island, thirty miles northeast, and Evans's destroyer was the closest to respond. Unencumbered by responsibility, DD-557 was shifted on the vinyl war board and chosen for this operation.

After performing his morning routine, Evans made his way to the combat information center, just four steps from his cabin. The ship was heading for a pass south of Mellu Island. Evans had been briefed on it days before. Several LSTs would pass ahead of them and aim to invade Mellu from the rear. Upon learning that all was going according to plan, Evans went to the bridge.

His steps rung dully on the steel steps as he ascended. His lee helmsman and helmsman were already waiting for him. Evans ordered them to idle and wait, allowing the LSTs time to form at the mouth of this pass. After half an hour, Evans ordered the *Johnston* southwest and watched three miles of northern Mellu beach glide by before reaching the mouth of the pass. The beach they had shelled the day before was visible off to port. The sand was cratered like the surface of the moon.

LSTs began moving as planned through the pass before the *Johnston* reached it, and Evans felt the urgency when he observed one Marine-laden tractor beach on a coral head.

Realizing that these waters were suddenly treacherous, Evans placed Lieutenant Elton Stirling and his executive officer, Lieutenant Commander Baker, on the roof of the bridge to give heads-up course changes. Below them his sonarmen sat in absolute silence behind the bridge, interpreting the pitch and depth of signals that registered off the reef walls below them.

As the *Johnston* moved through the pass, Hagen sat in the gun director, ready to swing the five-inch rifles out to meet resistance. Evans asked his radiomen to confirm that the heavy ships had paused their shelling. Once it was safe to enter the lagoon, the helmsman maneuvered north toward Namur.

As they began north, Bob Hagen quickly noticed the lack of targets and climbed down from the director for fresh air. Instead, though, Hagen found his captain standing at the foot of the ladder. Evans had intuited Hagen's desire to escape the blistering heat, so as he began talking to Hagen, he also took steps to starboard toward the open bridge wing. When they met on the disengaged side of the ship to prevent any snipers from having a shot at them, Evans explained to his gunnery officer that one of the bunkers they would find on Namur required special attention. The day before, several cruisers and battleships had failed to reduce this bunker to powder, but it was expected that the rearward-facing bulkheads of the bunker were not weak. Evans explained to Hagen that after immediate threats were dealt with, this bunker was to be reduced. Then Evans left Hagen to finish his smoke.

Soon Evans brought his destroyer to a halt two miles off the south coast of Namur Island. At 0840 he gave the order. Hagen's first two shots missed but a third squarely hit and fractured a smaller bunker. Dozens of Japanese men ran out after their refuge was hit and they, too, were cut down by the 40mm guns that stitched the beach. The tracer fire visible in the daylight was like drawing in the sand. The 40s would pound an area for a while and the large five-inch guns would rearrange the sand and clear the canvas. After the opening minutes, there was nothing left alive on the southwest quarter of the island.

All threats had been destroyed and Evans thought that now enough time was on hand to target the persistent bunker. Evans ordered the ship a little closer for a good shot. Seemingly everyone left alive had run there, and Evans ordered this redoubt to be tested from the rear.

Hagen let loose five rounds, observed no effect, and prepared to order another salvo. The bunker, however, "exploded in my face," Hagen remembered. Evans wrote in his after-action report: "Naturally a point of great interest was the scene of the explosion at 0952." It was obvious that only a couple inches of concrete had shielded this bunker's rear, and from the size of the blast, it was also clear that the bunker had been a magazine to house the island's artillery shells.

Evans's immediate astonishment was replaced with horror when he noticed an observation aircraft fall from the sky. Evans grabbed a radioman and hailed the captain of an LST. He covered an attempt to retrieve the pilot, but the LST was not quick enough.

After a moment of silence, Evans maneuvered his destroyer half a mile northwest, closing with the island and bringing its southeast portion into view. For over an hour, Evans landed shells where they were requested. At 1152 he ordered a cease-fire, and at 1157 American boots stepped ashore.

After the quick work done to Mellu and Namur, the *Johnston* was removed from the fire support role in the fight for Kwajalein. Evans might have begrudged this, but their war had just begun. He exited the lagoon the evening of February 1, came alongside the USS *Colorado* for fuel—a reminder of how far he had come from his days as an ensign aboard her—then assumed a position in the screen of a bombardment force north of Roi Island.

While patrolling outside the atoll, Evans followed the capture of its namesake, Kwajalein Island, on the fire support frequency. Evans was proud to see his young officers licking their chops as they listened to the barrage of requests for fire. Officers of the *Johnston* stood in the passageway outside the radio room, listening to frenetic requests for ammunition and medical support through the static crackle of voices rising above the sounds of gunfire. As a courtesy, Evans broadcast the fire support frequency over the public address system.

The next day, February 2, Evans learned that he had been named the commander of an attack group responsible for neutralizing Hollis Island to the northwest, but this unit was dissolved the next day after Evans's leaders assigned a different unit. Evans then spent the third through the fifth at anchor, inside Kwajalein Atoll.

Then he was unexpectedly ordered on the morning of the sixth of February to support a group of transports whose destination was the island of Tuvalu, seven hundred miles south of Kwajalein.

This trip would bring the *Johnston* south of the equator, spurring Evans to keep up with the "crossing the line" tradition. But the afternoon of the seventh, "Pollywogs revolted from the rule of the shellbacks upon learning that we were not crossing the line this time," Evans wrote. Instead, they went to investigate a sound contact north of the equator and broke off from the southbound transports. But Evans was unable to make contact through the night of the seventh, and then he was ordered to Majuro Atoll for fuel and ammunition on the morning of the eighth.

At Majuro Evans reported to Rear Admiral Jones's Service Squadron Ten for fuel, then spent two days unprofitably searching the atoll for an ammunition tender with five-inch shells to spare. He needed a resupply after the shelling of Mellu and Namur, but each possibility there was spoken for by a cruiser squadron. Evans's duty as a destroyer acting solo left him playing second fiddle to the needs of cruisers.

On the evening of the ninth, Evans prepared to leave for Kwajalein without having found ammunition, but hours earlier, while searching the atoll for an available ammunition ship, he had unknowingly sailed through a mass of jellyfish. These clogged his main condensers, caused overheating and ultimately engine failure.

The night of the ninth, the filter screens on the fire and bilge intakes were replaced every five minutes until the mass of jellyfish passed through the ship's engine cooling system. The problem was cured by sunrise on the tenth and Evans started back to Kwajalein. Upon sighting Kwajalein Atoll on the morning of the eleventh, Evans realized the cause for the competition for resources: During his absence from Kwajalein, an entirely new flotilla—Task Force 51, a troop transportation unit under Admiral Kelly Turner—had arrived. Its deployment required a slew of oil tankers and its escorting ships needed five-inch shells.

As Evans approached the atoll, he eyed this task force through his binoculars. Its size might have impressed him, but even more impressive was its timing. The task force had come less than three days after the atoll was fully captured. The logistical blunders of the Asiatic campaign were now ancient history. Evans must have wondered what would have happened had the Navy been this prepared at the beginning.

The *Johnston* was stopped short of entering the atoll. As the ship approached Kwajalein, a screening ship outside one of the deep-water entrances chimed in on the "talk between ships" (TBS) frequency. Evans learned that a submarine contact had been made to the west, and after confirming enough fuel was aboard, Evans took the job of hunting it. An afternoon of fruitless searching brought the *Johnston* to Gea Pass, a western entrance to Kwajalein. Here Evans patrolled through the night.

He was relieved in the morning by another destroyer and brought the *Johnston* into Kwajalein Atoll. Once inside the atoll, Evans attached to Kelly Turner's troop transports. This change of assignment did not lower the *Johnston*'s chance to see combat, but instead of bombardment, Evans would concern himself with antisubmarine warfare, screening the transports in a fashion similar to the role he had carried out while attached to the fleet support squadron as captain of the *Alden*. That night the crew slept inside Kwajalein's lagoon once again.

Without warning, the Klaxon signaled general quarters shortly after two in the morning—a response to tracer fire seen in the distance. Evans stepped into the CIC and listened to the TBS frequency of the engaged screening force, on which he heard that bombers were heading south for Roi Island. Evans would have known they intended to bomb either the airfield on Roi or the transports anchored inside the atoll.

Anticipating the latter, Evans maneuvered toward the transports and ordered his ship to make smoke, blocking out the moonlight and creating a thin gray layer above them. Now, with no clear view of the distant gunfire, the *Johnston*'s long-range radar was used to track a first and then a second group of approaching Japanese aircraft.

Though they never closed to within thirty miles, Evans likely did not sleep until the green blips on his radar screens vanished from sight. Men were rubbing their eyes when they woke up on Saturday morning. Fortunately, Evans wrote, the next two days were "very uneventful," and the crew were able to enjoy food provided by their Filipino cooks. Circulating among his sea cabin, the officers' wardroom, and his private cabin, Evans waited for information on the coming operations, read maps, and reflected on his bombardment work.

On the morning of February 14, preparation began for the capture of Eniwetok Atoll. Three hundred miles to the northwest, it is the second largest atoll in the Marshalls. Evans's destroyer was meant to sortie with the cruiser *Louisville*, the battleship *Colorado*, and the destroyers *Haggard* and *Hailey*, and together support a Marine invasion of Eniwetok's Parry Island.

The bombardment there lasted from their arrival on the eighteenth through the morning of the twenty-second, during which time the *Johnston* knocked out six pillboxes. Similarly to how Evans had maneuvered in Kwajalein, he brought his ship into the protected lagoon and bombarded from the rear. The isolated Japanese had not prepared for this. The defenses crumbled and the *Johnston* received no return fire while anchored less than five hundred yards from the beachhead. On the nineteenth alone, Evans loosed three hundred rounds of five-inch, sixteen hundred rounds of 40mm, and three thousand rounds of 20mm ammunition at Parry Island, and each day thereafter he maintained a similar rate of fire. Evans likely stayed awake most nights, observing star shells as they were launched. He finally left his position off Parry Island at midday on the twenty-third, then steamed to the wide entrance at the southwest of Eniwetok to relieve the destroyer *Hoel* of antisubmarine patrol.

Evans patrolled outside the atoll, then reported to Rear Admiral Davison's Task Group 51.6 and shifted to the screen of its carrier group on the twenty-fifth. Modern Hellcats and Dauntless dive-bombers made air strikes throughout Eniwetok Atoll, then returned to their flight decks each day before sunset, often genially tipping their wings to their screening ships before taking their turns in the landing patterns.

On March 1 Evans and Task Group 51.6 were ordered to Majuro Lagoon for rest. Evans remained until the sixth, and his crew enjoyed the downtime. It was the "first time since leaving San Diego condition four was set and the crew enjoyed relaxation and recreation." On March 7 the *Johnston* left with the carrier group, renamed Task Group 50.11, and headed south toward safer waters. The Marshalls were now firmly in Allied control. The carrier task group that Evans was sailing with was being recalled to a secret location, but Evans inferred that his destination was either Espiritu Santo or Funafuti lagoon at Tuvalu. Either destination would have them cross the equator.

On March 8, the force did cross, and "at 1400 Neptunus Rex and the Royal Party came aboard and initiation ceremonies for all slimy pollywogs were held in accordance with ancient tradition," Evans wrote. A welcome distraction, King Neptune received hundreds more shellbacks into his ranks.

———

On March 12, Evans anchored at Espiritu Santo, Vanuatu—back where he had dropped off the New Zealand construction battalion aboard the *Alden* two years earlier. Upon arriving, Task Group 50.11 was dissolved and Evans reported to Destroyer Squadron 94 of Admiral William F. "Bull" Halsey's Third Fleet. At Vanuatu Evans likely spent time with his maps, carefully fingering through sketches of the Southwest Pacific. In the officers' wardroom on the table were sketches of islands in the Caroline group, New Ireland, and the holdings in the Admiralty Islands and in the islands west of New Guinea. Each of these would be visited by the American military in the coming months.

At Vanuatu the *Johnston* was dry-docked. Evans oversaw maintenance of his sonar equipment, and an anticorrosive coat of paint was applied to his ship's underside. Outside of this ship-related work, Evans likely also sought out a wide range of opinions. On the island, commanders certainly speculated. It was felt that the Mariana and Caroline Islands were the next targets. Evans walked around Vanuatu, gathering information about his future task. It was clear that he would be employed in a carrier screen in either location; the islands that they would assault were orders of magnitude larger than any in the Marshalls, so they would need to be attacked by aircraft. Evans could clearly see near a dozen carriers offshore—a thrilling testament that the United States' industrial might must surely overwhelm the Japanese.

Young pilots practiced carrier landings in the safety of the waters off Vanuatu as Evans's crew watched captivated for eight days. Then, on March 20, the *Johnston* was ordered to Purvis Bay, Florida Island, in the Solomon Island group. On the public address system that morning, Evans explained the movement. They were going to fuel up at Purvis Bay and prepare for a push north with Task Force 50. In other words, they were moving a few hundred miles closer to Japan, and they had to keep an eye out for submarines.

Corpses of warships littered the ocean floor off Purvis Bay—hence the reason it was named Iron Bottom Sound. Evans did not have to wait long among the ghosts of those warships, though. After arriving on the twenty-second of March, he left again on the morning of the twenty-fourth with the destroyer *Trathen*. The pair maneuvered to meet a destroyer squadron near New Ireland, several hundred miles farther north, east of Papua New Guinea. There, they would search for Japanese shipping. This was a unique hunter-killer role that Evans relished. They seemed to be pushing north ahead of the larger task force. While the carriers gathered themselves to the south for a push into the Mariana and Caroline Islands, *Johnston* and *Trathen* would be the tip of the spear.

En route to their patrolling station on the morning of the twenty-fifth, lookouts sighted two Japanese transports anchored offshore of New Ireland's southern tip. Hagen was ready with the guns. Evans shrewdly knew to remind his sonarmen to listen for submarine contact. This could be a trap.

General quarters was called as soon as the lookouts spotted the transports, and before the targets got much closer, men manned the 40mm guns, their barrels swung out to starboard. Evans was sweeping the scene, his instincts telling him to expect the unexpected. After the *Johnston* closed in, these transports proved to be beached and abandoned.

For another two days, Evans patrolled the waters around New Ireland, a thousand miles to the southwest of the recently captured Marshall Islands, but all Japanese assets had long since been abandoned or moved north. After finding nothing, Evans received new orders to move north to the Caroline Islands. On March 28, Evans anchored on station off Kapingamarangi Atoll and worked for the next twenty-four hours shelling enemy strongpoints there. Men sang songs belowdecks as they doggedly hauled shells onto the hydraulic lifts while the guns above them boomed. "An observation tower, several blockhouses, pillboxes, and dugouts along the beach were shelled," Evans wrote. This was all completed by the morning of March 29.

The next set of orders brought the *Johnston* to Empress Augusta Bay, Bougainville Island—the easternmost holding of Papua New Guinea—five hundred miles south of the Caroline Islands. Once captured, Bougainville would provide American Army pilots a base from which to fly. The *Johnston* arrived off Bougainville Island the morning of the thirtieth and awaited the arrival of three Army

observers from the 14th Army Corps to come aboard and help
manage the bombardment of an airfield on Bougainville Island,
near Cape Torokina. The prospect of contributing to the capture
of an airfield gave rise to new excitement. The next morning three
Army officers—a colonel and two lieutenants—came aboard.

After a two-hour mission, Evans's personal gig was lowered
into the drink to return the three Army officers to their camp by
the afternoon of March 31. The result of the conference was that
the *Johnston* reduced several entrenched hideouts along the edge
of the airfield. Evans then removed his destroyer from the shoal
waters around the island and patrolled nearby until returning to
Cape Torokina, Bougainville, on April 2 to take aboard an Army
major and his staff. This ensemble teamed up for bombardment
as well. Working in tandem with a spotting plane, the *Johnston* sent
244 rounds of five-inch ammunition toward a supply area about
a thousand yards inland, east of the Takessi River.

The results of cooperation with the Army liaisons spoke for
themselves. Upon completion of this second mission, an Army
observation plane relayed that "the area has been well covered,
looks like it has been all shot to hell, looks like a job well done."
Before Evans's coxswain dropped the major back ashore, Evans
received a request for help. His crew and he were needed to search
a grid southwest of the island to hunt for a submarine. The crew
remained at general quarters for the next twenty-four hours. On
the third of April, the hunt was given up, though not before thirteen depth charges were dropped throughout the night.

Evans rejoined his squadron and after patrolling as a unit off
Bougainville's southern shore, this division was relieved and given
orders to steam to the Solomon Islands for rest and relaxation. By

the fourth, they reached their destination. Upon reaching Florida Island the unit was greeted from the air by flights of naval aviators. In this watery sanctuary, they waited for orders until April 8.

Guadalcanal was just over the horizon, and the men were keenly aware of and sobered by the proximity of the scene of the horrendous naval losses incurred there in 1942. Nevertheless, this was a recreational rest, and sailors took rafts to the beach as they pleased. Men who remained aboard played cards. Sailors swam and some fished. What they caught with large sticks and chicken wire hooks was completely unknown to them because it was unlike anything they had pulled from their childhood rivers and lakes. Many wrote letters, hopeful that they would have an opportunity to send them home. Some men boxed to keep their sanity. Aside from this, a sailor could stare out at the ocean and simply appreciate the beauty of the place.

During a routine haircut on a day of calm seas at Purvis Bay, Evans informed his barber, Edward Block, that though locals had traded them the outrigger canoe they had been using, they needed to get rid of it before they resumed wartime patrol. With measured tone, Evans acknowledged its use as a tool for fun, but in the busy weeks to come, his men had better remove all extra equipment tied onto the deck. The canoe would be a hazard should it catch fire during a coming operation. Block agreed. "It was fun while it lasted," he remembered. And through it all, pilots from the nearby carriers practiced and practiced their takeoffs and landings.

On April 9, the *Johnston* was assigned to Carrier Division 24—a role that promised Evans and his men would have watchful nights on anti-submarine patrol. Their first days out from Purvis

Bay were routine, though heavy rain on the tenth threatened to send rookie pilots skidding off the flight deck. During this "ticklish hour" of heavy rain, Evans wrote, groups of his men kept near their life rafts should any pilots crash.

From the bridge Evans watched the carriers in the distance. The engines of the Grumman Wildcats were faint in Evans's ears at a distance of a couple miles. The rain was strong. Individual aircraft were visible only after they were well into the descent onto the carrier's flight deck. As each aircraft made its approach, all half expected one of the pilots to miss a wire and slide into the ocean or belly-roll into the superstructure. The pilots' incessant training, however, proved its worth and there were no incidents.

On April 11, the carrier group reached the Bismarck Archipelago. Here the *Johnston* escorted the carriers while their air wings flew to soften targets and cover Army landings on Emirau Island. The *Johnston* remained in this escort role until the nineteenth, then was called on to escort two merchant ships traveling a hundred fifty miles due west to Manus in the Admiralty Island chain. The *Johnston* arrived on April 20 with the two merchant vessels and began back east toward Emirau Island to resume screening operations, proceeding independently to a patrolling station fifteen miles northeast of there.

The carriers were still operating there upon Evans's return, though the carrier-based Wildcats were not the only aircraft in the skies. Heavy B-24s began flying from constructed airstrips shortly after Evans left to escort the merchant ships west to Manus, and the big silver bombers were clearly visible as they moved to and from the island. A bombing effort on the Caroline and Palau Islands had begun.

Through the end of April and the start of May, the *Johnston* continued escorting various ships to New Caledonia and the Solomon Islands and back to the islands off the eastern coast of New Guinea, such as Manus and Emirau. This period was "sheer boredom for us," Bob Hagen recalled, and he spoke for most of the crew.

They were going through the motions, but having been in the combat zone under Evans's command for four months, his crew had learned a lot. He'd had a particularly high impact on his officers, many of whom were gaining valuable experience that could lead to promotions. One in particular, Lieutenant Elton Stirling, was due for a promotion to executive officer at the end of May because Lieutenant Commander Howard Baker was set to leave the *Johnston*. With this promotion looming, Lieutenant Stirling seemed to tighten up. He was securing his reputation as a disciplinarian in anticipation for his promotion to XO, though during this long period of uneventful patrolling through tamed waters, the crew found the extra discipline unnecessary. Evans agreed with them. One night when Evans knew they were bound to find no enemy, he brought a beer to Lieutenant Stirling, who was standing watch on the bridge. Thinking it was a trick, Stirling left the beer sitting where Evans placed it. However, a few days later, he held the same watch, and Evans brought the beer back, then softly declared that "this better not be here in the morning." Whether the beer was thrown overboard or drunk is unknown, but the next day Evans was satisfied. The incident exemplified his style: The message was delivered and no harshness exchanged.

The boredom was not limited to the officers. One night between midnight and 0400, Evans took a walk. Edward Block, the ship's barber, was also the gun captain for a 20mm mount, and he had allowed his crew to fall asleep during the first watch. Evans's voice reached Block before the gunner saw him. "Who is the gun captain here?" Evans asked from within a shadow. When Block replied that he was, Evans stepped out and asked, "Do you know these men are sleeping?" Block replied that he did. "The captain gave me hell but in a nice way," Block recalled.

The six weeks spent escorting merchant ships among the islands of the Southwest Pacific blended together, but wherever Evans interacted with his men, they remembered the event. Despite the anticipation that something would happen, nothing went on. However, on the sixteenth of May, while escorting American merchant vessels off the coast of Papua New Guinea, an aircraft spotted a submarine and vectored the *Johnston* toward it.

The shrieking Klaxon brought every sailor to his position, and as his ship came to life, Evans would have made his way to the bridge. Belowdecks, the crackle of the radio reverberated throughout the combat information center and Lieutenant Stirling worked on the vinyl board to figure out the scene.

On the radio with a spotter aircraft, Evans learned that multiple submarines were in the area, so he "continued operations northeast of Buka Island searching for submarines reported by aircraft," Evans typed. Throughout the evening of the sixteenth, he ordered more than a dozen depth charges into the sea, and the hunt continued into the early hours of the seventeenth. The crew remained at general quarters overnight. Evans stayed on the bridge monitoring the efforts of the sonarmen and the young sailors on watch, and by 0200, it was clear that oil was on the surface of the water.

By dawn an oil slick almost a mile wide surfaced. Evans patrolled its perimeter through midday. By the evening neither Evans's sonarmen nor the spotter plane had sighted a submarine. It should have surfaced for air, so the *Johnston* was credited with the kill.

Cheers of praise were still ringing throughout the ship when Evans finished his congratulatory public address in the morning and ordered full steam to Guadalcanal. They had urgent orders to join a carrier task group. Then they would start for the Marshall Islands.

By June 8, the *Johnston* was back at Kwajalein Atoll, waiting for forces of the Fifth Fleet to gather. A large offensive was coming. The target of the American Navy was the Mariana Islands, thirteen hundred miles west of the Marshalls.

After five days the Fifth Fleet was ready to sortie. It took twelve hours for all the ships to leave their anchorage in the expansive Kwajalein Atoll and gather outside in the open ocean. By the evening of the thirteenth, they were ready. Two groups formed outside Kwajalein: the Saipan and the Guam invasion forces.

Evans was assigned to the latter. This flotilla of carriers, battleships, cruisers, and destroyers arrived at their preinvasion station off Guam on June 16. East of Guam, they waited. Heading west during the day and retiring east at night, the fleet stalked back and forth, waiting for invasion day.

Meanwhile, the invasion of Saipan went forward. It was a period of great anxiety for everyone involved. The Japanese were settling in. The invasions had been meant to be conducted simultaneously, though greater resistance on Saipan was met than expected and this caused the leadership to decide to indefinitely postpone the Guam invasion from June 18. This order kept the invasion fleet at sea longer than expected, and on July 2, the tension was broken when the force was ordered back to the Marshall Islands. The unexpectedly stubborn battle for Saipan convinced the Navy that the Army's 77th Division, which was not yet in theater, would be needed on Guam.

The task force returned to Kwajalein and waited for thirteen days. Routine maintenance was kept up, PT drills were held on the fantail, and films were watched on the quarterdeck at night. The *Johnston* remained anchored with the naval bombardment force until the seventeenth of July. With the 77th Division resting in their transports north of Guam, Evans weighed anchor to join them. In the screen of carrier Task Group 53.2, Evans proceeded to Guam. William-Day—Guam's invasion designation—was nearly at hand.

Task Group 53.2 returned to the waters off Guam in the predawn hours of July 21. Evans left the carriers around dawn and took station in Agat Bay, a couple miles from shore, and here the armada gathered. Dozens of troop transports gathered farther out to sea, off the *Johnston*'s port side. The Marines rocked in the waves, checking and double-checking their gear. More than fifty thousand men of the 3rd Amphibious Corps lay floating in their steel transports. Nested like Russian matryoshka dolls, the landing ship docks (LSDs) offshore each held a thousand men, and within these LSDs were the landing craft infantry (LCIs), each packed tight with hundreds of Marines. Among them were also dozens of landing craft mechanized (LCMs). These carried Sherman tanks, which were essential for the jungle warfare that the Marines would find on Guam. Between the *Johnston* and the gathering of transports, off to their right, battleships wallowed in a row, their broadsides trained on the beach, their fourteen-inch guns extending over the sides like a wall of pikes. The *Johnston* was positioned closer to shore, underneath the guns of six American battlewagons.

When the sun rose on July 21, there were also eight cruisers, thirty-two destroyers, and three carriers offshore. Everything was still but for the voices of nearly a hundred thousand Marines and sailors as they murmured among themselves.

The island of Guam is roughly thirty miles long and largely covered in dense jungle canopy. This great fleet was gathered off its southwestern portion. The island, about five miles at its widest southern portion, tapered off to the north, with a mountainous region that was about two miles wide. On its southwestern shore, about ten miles from the island's base, is a mile-long peninsula that juts out into the sea. This peninsula held an airstrip, as well as high ground used by Japanese artillery units. The beach around this peninsula, one portion to the north and the other to its south, was the target of the landing forces.

Offshore, the 3rd Marine Division and the 1st Provisional Brigade waited, along with the 77th Division. This campaign for Guam was the beginning of the end and both sides knew it. The fighting would be brutal, and Evans certainly made sure his men knew this. Their job in softening the Japanese strongpoints would save lives.

CHAPTER 8

The Finest Bombardment Ship in the Fleet

JULY 1944–AUGUST 1944

W-Day came on July 21 at 0530 when the USS *Colorado* began firing her secondary battery of five-inch guns toward the beachhead. At 0543 the *Pennsylvania* joined in. Then Hagen climbed into the gun director.

At 0550 the *Johnston* joined with her five-inch guns and 40mm mounts. The concussion of a single gun slowly turned into rapid fire. The lighter rapid fire of the 40s was separated by the deeper boom of the main guns. The sea around the *Johnston* was disturbed by the firing of the battleships behind her when they opened up with their main batteries, the *Colorado*'s sixteen-inch guns and the *Pennsylvania*'s fourteen-inch. The shock of those guns was enough to throw sailors off their feet. Water lapped against the disengaged side of Evans's ship.

At 0602 Evans was ordered to retire south of the *Pennsylvania* because the guns of this battleship had grown so hot, her skipper feared an accidental discharge. These older battleships had to lower their guns to load the heavy shells. Since the breaches became so hot, a premature discharge could have blown the *Johnston* out of the water. Evans realized the logic in moving but he did utter a few choice words for having to remove his guns at the start of the shooting.

Hagen climbed down from the director to escape the heat and found Evans searching through binoculars. To his captain, Hagen mentioned his own sighting of a group of blockhouses and bunkers on the beach beyond Agat Bay. Evans acknowledged his gunnery officer by handing him the binoculars and sharing his discovery of a church on the beachhead left over from American missionary work. Through his binoculars he could see the top of a cross. Evans and Hagen concluded that the church was a headquarters for the Japanese defense. Made of stone and surrounded by the jungle, it was a perfect hideout.

Soon the *Pennsylvania* captain radioed Evans and told him to assume his old position closer into the beach. Evans responded to the crackling voice on the radio by relating the sighting of the church on the beach. At 0610 Evans moved back in and resumed shooting.

Hagen fought back with their forward two guns, sending one-shot salvos every thirty seconds. Japanese soldiers were observed running on the beach, abandoning their artillery positions for the jungle. The reprieve in return fire—the Japanese landed shells a hundred yards in front of the *Johnston*—gave Hagen time to land shells on the church, though all he accomplished was knocking loose stacked-up coral.

At 0615 Evans ordered a cease-fire and went belowdecks to see the work done by the officers in the CIC. With no surprise Evans found that Lieutenant Stirling, his executive officer, had added intensively to their map of Guam, marking targets sent down to him by spotter aircraft. After a few minutes Evans returned to the bridge.

Through binoculars Evans could see the details of the defense from one mile out. The beach was short but the tree line had already retreated twenty yards after the initial bombardment. The Marines would use the room created to avoid presighted artillery traps. Still, in the remaining dense jungle, Japanese artillery was hidden, so at 0618 Evans gave Hagen orders to set the 40mm gunners loose and to resume firing single five-inch salvos every minute. The large guns went to work dislodging the Japanese from their position in the old church, while the 40mm gun batteries attacked the tree line.

For nearly twenty minutes, Evans watched his guns fail to reduce the church to rubble. Then he sent word to the captain of the *Pennsylvania*. This ghost of Pearl Harbor would use fourteen-inch rifles for the job. At 0640 Evans was given the gift of watching a three-quarter-ton shell land, and he realized why they were called "haymakers." The first shot removed enough coral and stacked logs to reveal the original walls of that holy place. The next three shells killed the soldiers inside.

By 0650 the *Johnston* had shot nearly one hundred rounds of main battery shells and continued searching for targets of opportunity, working along the area of beach marked for the Marine landings. Hagen moved between pillboxes and bunkers, rarely allowing more than ten minutes to pass before yelling, "Changing target," and sending another twenty rounds at a suspected strongpoint. The structure of the old church had fallen but still gunners from *Johnston*'s antiaircraft mounts strafed it, hoping to catch Japanese soldiers running between cover.

Evans scoured his maps. Soon they would be asked to address the artillery positions on Orote Peninsula. From this flanking position, artillery guns would easily be able to shell the Marines as they landed. The peninsula stuck out into the sea, taunting its attackers. Belowdecks, the men in the handling rooms loaded rounds onto their hydraulic hoists, knowing that Hagen would use them well.

To get a good angle on this position, Evans moved his destroyer in close. As he did, guns from this position began shooting at him. The *Johnston*'s bow was under a half mile from the beach, bobbing in four-foot waves and drawing all the fire while the Marines prepared their approach.

The topography of the cliffs limited the Japanese range of motion and speed; they could not change targets quickly. Shells were landing around the *Johnston*, but Evans could maneuver before the Japanese fixed their aim. The return fire from Hagen was impressive. Hagen would land a hit, then yell, "Changing target!" and the men in the gun mounts would surrender control to Hagen, who'd synchronously move the turrets, release them from his control, and allow the gun captains to work while he looked for the next target.

In the Marshall Islands, both Hagen and Evans had noticed the fluorescent blue color that Japanese powder created when burned. Now they used it to identify targets, though it took a keen eye. Amid the smoke of the burning jungle, the blue hint that rose up was harder to notice, but it was a sure sign of a concealed artillery piece.

As W Hour neared, Hagen turned his attention from Orote Peninsula and began working over the southern landing beach again. At 0800 Hagen again looked to the church, whose structure was visible after the *Pennsylvania* had removed the heavy layers of coral, logs, and overgrowth earlier that morning. The jungle was being stripped away, revealing rows of sandbag bunkers and artillery emplacements.

At 0822 landing craft crept toward the beachhead, snaking through the bombardment ships that were ahead of them. Before the LSIs and LCMs got close, the bombardment fleet began a final barrage. The deep synchronized thuds of the battleships' fourteen-inch ordnance echoed across Agat Bay. Cruisers and destroyers followed suit. The Japanese were not expected to recover for several minutes.

The 22nd and the 4th Marine Regiments landed across four beaches on Agat Bay that stretched over a mile. In the distance, artillery pieces were hidden in dense jungle and resilient sandstone caves, and an even more formidable defensive position flanked the landings on the Agat beach to the north. This was Orote Peninsula, the first objective of the campaign.

The gun crews of the *Johnston* fired 368 five-inch rounds in the eight minutes before a cease-fire was ordered at 0830. Once the echoes of heavy guns dissipated, the sounds of dozens of small engines revving up were all that remained. At 0831 boots hit the ground in a display of guts and discipline.

The Japanese on the beach were initially stunned, but troops held in protected reserves rushed to sandbagged defenses. At 0832 Evans resumed firing, sending two three-gun salvos toward Agat Bay's shoreline per minute. Quickly the Marines pushed forward, and Evans waited anxiously for his radio operators to establish contact with the landing force.

This came at 0850. One deck below the bridge, sailors were listening when a Marine radio operator came through the static, screaming above the sound of his comrades' gunfire. That the *Johnston* had secured contact with the spotters onshore within twenty minutes of their landing was a testament to Evans's insistence on training.

Destroyers thrive in close-support roles. Evans's smaller guns and shallow draft gave him the ability to provide surgical precision. It is dangerous work. Long-range naval bombardment is known as "plunging fire," but fire to aid troops from a short distance has a flat trajectory and slices anything in its path. It has an effect similar to clearing a path through a dense jungle with dynamite.

In the combat information center, Lieutenant Stirling continued to keep up with the fire support frequency, marking on his map the locations of individual companies and advancing tanks. His work was important because once Marines got off the beach, the shooting became tricky.

Thirty-four minutes into the battle, and six minutes after gaining contact with fire support units, Marines called on Evans to fire on a concentration of troops counterattacking their position a hundred yards from the beachhead. First, Hagen released one white phosphorus round. Then, with the area marked, he let loose five full five-gun salvos in rapid fire. Seconds passed with no word from the Marines, though the confused voices of the other fire control operators on the other bombardment ships came through the shared frequency. Then came the declaration "Target destroyed, beautiful shooting."

Hagen continued to receive targets. He would yell, "Changing targets," the cue for his gun captains to disengage their turrets and prepare to swing in line with his direction. The Marines would request a white phosphorus round to mark guns hidden in dense foliage and tree cover or to mark areas of troop concentration, and then the battleships and cruisers would commence rapid-fire shelling.

After silencing the Japanese counterattack just before 0900, Evans ordered a cease-fire. The silence was broken at 0915 when the crew members of a four-inch cannon revealed themselves and took a shot at the *Johnston*. The shell missed by a hundred yards and Hagen determined that it had come from the south of Orote Peninsula. A second shot missed and confirmed the location to Hagen, who sent five three-gun salvos toward it with no effect. The sixth salvo hit an ammunition dump nearby, clearing the gun and all of the trees in that area. By 0930 the Marines were several hundred yards past the beachhead, which had been reduced to a mess of burned obstacles, craters, and reduced bunkers. Beyond the beach the dense jungle seemed inviting. The Marines entering it would have no escape for many days.

Evans would follow the movement of his forward two guns, then climb down to the radio shack or the CIC to listen to the appraisal of their work by the Marines ashore. If Evans was not on the bridge or the port bridge wing getting fresh air or down in the mess hall having coffee and fresh bread, then he was in the radio shack or in the CIC with his XO, Elton Stirling.

Evans observed the tank movements on their map of the island with particular intensity. They were tough to keep up with; once the tanks got off the beach and entered the jungle, their movements were reported as accurately as possible by aircraft. Evans would document his frustration at this difficulty that night as he began his after-action report. Often the Marine tanks would push ahead of the ground troops, causing confusion among the bombardment ships.

Through the rest of the morning, the *Johnston* provided fire support, sending white phosphorus rounds and five-inch shells screaming into the jungle. Overhead aircraft launched rockets as a way of guiding the larger gunfire. It was like Armageddon. At 1125 Evans observed with horror an F4U Corsair crash on Orote Peninsula.

At 1520 a general cease-fire was ordered on the *Johnston*, but the crew remained at general quarters until 1730. Sunset came at 1915, and men gathered to watch it on the *Johnston's* disengaged side. As men smoked cigarettes in safe places on deck, the western horizon turned black. Then it was lights out. By the end of the first day, the Marines had pushed a mile inland, and they held a two-mile-wide front.

Many men would work through the night, distinguishing themselves in their roles. Lieutenant Stirling was one of those men. The *Johnston's* XO would remain awake all night, arranging a target deck for the morning and giving Hagen, himself pulling an all-nighter in the gun director, the assignments for that night; mostly they fired star shells for the soldiers rather than providing direct fire support. However, despite the darkness the shooting did not stop. Hagen sent two-gun salvos toward Guam every quarter hour.

It was not the noise that kept the crew awake, but the terrible effects that their flashless powder bags had on the *Johnston's* ventilation system. The excess grit left over after a gun blast from the flashless powder clogged the ventilation ducts. The debris in the ventilation system ignited a fire and reactively the system was turned off each time the guns were fired. The crew's quarters became an oven for the rest of the campaign. Throughout the ship, portholes were opened and remained so.

Evans woke on the twenty-second well before the Marines onshore had breakfast. He made sure his officers were awake and alert. After securing from general quarters at 0600, he held a rapid-fire meeting in the officers' wardroom. At the same time each morning, they would be briefed on the progress of the Marines the day before, and officers would be able to address issues they had noticed over the previous twenty-four hours. This first morning after W-Day, the chief concern was the shutdown of the ship's ventilation system and the possibility of heatstrokes, though by the end of this first week of combat, the officers of the *Johnston* would give their captain lists of recommendations they had for future operations.

Before any men—tired, half awake, and forgetting they were in a combat zone—stepped outside for cooler air, officers on watch pulled them back inside. Soon all of the crew would be alert. The second day of combat began without ceremony. Shore batteries on Orote Peninsula fired at the *Johnston* but all missed.

The first requests for fire support came at 0857, but at 0905 a cease-fire was ordered because the tanks had moved position overnight and their locations were unknown. Once the tanks' positions were confirmed, the shooting began again. Evans had contact with a Marine radio operator ashore. On the morning of the twenty-second, this Marine requested that Evans bombard the southeastern end of the peninsula heavily in order to flush the Japanese toward their lines. Then, by the afternoon, close-fire support was requested. Several times fire was checked because it landed too close to the Marine positions, but on many more occasions throughout the day, the fighting required these types of risk.

The *Johnston* remained in position in Agat Bay—south of Orote Peninsula—for seven more days. The main objective was to neutralize the peninsula. The forces that Evans helped land south of the peninsula, the 77th Division and the 1st Brigade of the Marines, were responsible for capturing it. They would isolate and besiege the Japanese soldiers on the peninsula. To the north of the peninsula, the 3rd Marine Division would form a front line through the island's midsection and wait for the peninsula to be captured before moving toward mountain strongpoints in the island's north.

On the peninsula the Japanese had thousands of soldiers, an airfield, and guns that looked down on Agat Bay. As historian Samuel Eliot Morison wrote, "Orote was a natural target for naval gunfire, and the Navy gave it all it had, pounding selected positions for 30 minutes to an hour every morning while the Marines were eating breakfast." It had to be captured before continuing north.

July 22 and 23 were intense days of bombardment. The *Johnston*'s deck was covered with empty brass shells by the end of each day. Over these first three days, Evans overused his guns, ignoring his prescribed allotment of ammunition. Despite being reminded of the shortage by his quartermaster, Evans kept giving it to the

Japanese. When he got on the radio to request more ammunition, his superiors deferred his requests. Refusing to wait, he boarded his wooden captain's gig and motored over to a supply ship farther out to sea, then demanded what shells he needed. Smiling to himself as he came back aboard his destroyer, Evans then went alongside the supply ship and took aboard more than eight hundred five-inch shells on the evening of the twenty-second.

By the morning of the twenty-fourth, it was apparent that the Japanese on Orote Peninsula would put up stubborn resistance. This evening the *Johnston* came close to shore, firing her 40mm guns at soldiers manning artillery pieces on the peninsula's high ground. The Marines inched their way west, pushing the Japanese toward the end of the peninsula, but the Japanese positions east of the old American base on the peninsula, held them back. Evans had six casualties brought aboard the afternoon of the twenty-fourth. Then he was given a special assignment: A few hard-to-reach artillery guns had to be neutralized.

On the evening of the twenty-fourth at high tide, Evans maneuvered his destroyer into the armpit between Neye Island and Pelagi Rock. Guns tucked inside caves on the north side of Neye Island, separated from the peninsula on the south side by less than a hundred yards, prevented Marines from advancing any farther. Whether Evans volunteered or his card was pulled is unknown, but his crew was trusted with this task. With the tide up, Evans brought his destroyer within fifty yards of the beach in order to target the artillery on Neye Island.

Evans paid special attention to his lee helmsman, the sailor who controlled the ship's power lever, because in the push and pull of the tide, the *Johnston* was at high risk of beaching. Evans ordered one engine room to spin its screw in reverse while the other spun its screw clockwise to forward thrust. This kept the *Johnston* jockeying back and forth, and its propellers in deep water. These constricted waters were one problem. Another problem was the range.

To get an angle on the caves that hid these guns, and with the *Johnston* so close inshore, the target was too far underneath the nose of the ship's forward-most five-inch gun. Gun 51 could hit the cave on Neye Island only when the tide pulled back and allowed the *Johnston's* bow to dip.

Time was another problem. The high tide would drop soon, and Evans observed Japanese gunners reoccupying their positions following each direct hit his gun made. The defenders knew the position's importance and hoped to hang onto it long enough for high tide to drop and force the Americans to wait another day before attacking it again. The Marines ashore could not safely seize the western two-thirds of Orote Peninsula without this island first being neutralized. Japanese defenders desperately tried to turn back Evans's destroyer with small-arms fire. Their bullets bounced off the armored bridge, but neither the officers on the bridge nor the men they led were distracted from their work.

Men in 40mm mounts engaged individual defenders while the crew of gun 51 tested their skills and independently fought this sheltered artillery piece. After an hour the *Johnston* landed a hit that completely destroyed the gun and removed it as a threat. The receding tide failed to beach Evans's ship before his lee helmsman ordered both engines back full. The night of the twenty-fourth, the *Johnston's* crew slept better knowing that they had contributed considerably to the removal of the Japanese from Orote Peninsula.

The next morning, the Marines were glad not to be accosted by gunfire from Neye Island, though they still did not wish to rush forward. They requested the *Johnston* to shell Japanese positions and force the enemies to leave their hiding places and attack, rather than leave the Marines to dig them out.

By the afternoon of the twenty-fifth, the Japanese were desperate. The commander of the forces trapped on Orote Peninsula "ordered his men to make a frontal attack, preparing them for the sacrifice by issuing all the beer, sake and synthetic Scotch on the peninsula—and there was plenty; Guam seems to have been a liquor supply center for the Japanese," Samuel Eliot Morison wrote. In his memoir of events on the island, Marine Frank Hough wrote that "sake crazed troops boiled out of Mangrove cover on the front of the 3rd Battalion 22nd Marine Regiment, led by sword swinging and flag-waving officers, the troops carrying sticks, pitchforks, baseball bats and empty bottles in addition to their rifles."

After the Japanese losses sustained following their banzai charge on Marine defenses, the picture on the ground changed often. Aboard the *Johnston* in the CIC, Elton Stirling kept up with the Japanese defense. It was softening under pressure from the Marines. Evans often visited his XO in the CIC, bringing him coffee as his reward for remaining awake nearly four consecutive days. Together the men studied the progress made by the Marines on Orote Peninsula; still four more days were needed to remove those Japanese dug in there.

One sailor was wounded by a lucky ricochet, but up to this point, the crew had not had a casualty despite small-arms fire peppering the deck and superstructure. This would change, though, because the ship's doctor had offered to tend wounded Marines. The barber, Ed Block, wrote in his journal that "to see those young kids laying there all shot up brought tears to my eyes and I cried. But for the grace of God I could have been one of those kids." Evans, too, felt a connection to the Marines on the island. He had gotten to know how they lived while sailing aboard the *Chaumont*. The sight of wounded Marines being operated on in the officers' wardroom gave Evans and the entire crew a refreshed sense of purpose about the job they were doing in fire support. During the final days of bombardment on Orote Peninsula, the *Johnston* was very close to shore. After one intense bombardment, passion overtook one of the junior officers on the bridge. Lieutenant Welch wielded his .45 service pistol and waged his own war on the Japanese. He fired even after Evans demanded that he stop, apparently deaf from the concussion of the *Johnston*'s gunfire. Welch reloaded and kept firing his revolver until Evans got directly in his ear and yelled, "Damn it, Welch, cease fire!" Welch did and turned around to face the men on the bridge, grinning from ear to ear.

By dawn of the twenty-ninth, the northern and southern forces joined their lines. Orote Peninsula was nearly captured; only a company was needed to complete that operation. As Evans studied the moves, which were repeated on the chessboard in CIC, it took only until the afternoon for American tanks to secure the peninsula. From Agat Bay, Evans could see American flags on top of the tanks that traveled to the western tip of the peninsula.

Farther inland the other Marine units were also having success. By nightfall Evans was belowdecks in the CIC with his XO talking through the details of the Marines' progress east. Mounts Chachao and Alutom had been captured by the 3rd Marine Division and Mount Tenjo by the 77th.

Upon realizing that the Marines had captured Orote Peninsula, Evans got on the loudspeaker and congratulated his crew members who were unable to come on deck. Their cheers rose from within the ship and were clearly heard on the bridge. Evans was thrilled. His destroyer had been the closest to shore in the bombardment fleet.

Evans was overwhelmed with joy, but he knew what to do with himself; his crew and he needed rest. From the evening of the twenty-ninth to the morning of the thirty-first, the men on the *Johnston* received downtime. They performed submarine patrols farther out to sea where the danger was negligible. Evans knew this job was an excuse to get time off; there was no need for a screen because Japanese submarines could not have pulled off an attack when three carriers were on station to provide anti-submarine patrols.

Before sunset on the thirty-first, the *Johnston* left Orote Peninsula, sailed around Guam's northern end, and stationed herself here with the destroyer USS *Guest* and the heavy cruiser USS *New Orleans*. Evans screened the efforts of these ships only while they labored to soften up the Japanese defenses around the Marines' next objective, Mount Santa Rosa. Evans eyed this objective. It rose six hundred feet and lay three-quarters of a mile beyond the two-hundred-foot cliffs that rose out of the ocean. There was no beach and this allowed the bombardment ships to get close to shore, set in between the *Johnston* and Guam.

Northern Guam still held thousands of Japanese troops but

the jungle growth would slow the Marines down. So the initial shelling the units gave was southwest of Mount Santa Rosa. The gunfire was used to cut down jungle growth, making an approach to Mount Santa Rosa that the Marines could use. It was an important objective. Any advance to the north toward Ritidian and Pati Points had to be prefaced by an assault there. Japanese troops positioned there would have torn apart the right flank of any Marines looking to attack farther up toward the northern tip of the island. After a couple days of providing a submarine screen for the bombardment force, the *Johnston* joined in, firing west of Mount Santa Rosa in the morning hours of August 2. By nightfall on the third, Evans's guns had sent four thousand five-inch rounds at Guam. That night the *Johnston* was removed entirely from a bombardment role. Two battleships and an additional cruiser were brought in because their larger guns could easily reach the island's northern areas that needed shelling. This left the *Johnston* and four other destroyers that had also joined to assume a screening role.

Evans watched from a distance as ships pounded the ground in front of the Marines' approach to Mount Santa Rosa. After a couple days, Marines arrived at the base of this mountain and began ascending its steep western slope, every foot taking determination and naval firepower. On August 5, Santa Rosa was captured and the attack rolled north. Action reports returned stating that the 77th Division suffered only forty-one killed or missing and 104 wounded. "That such very light casualties were incurred in storming a major strong point was due largely to the intensive naval shelling," wrote Evans, bragging of his crew in his own after-action report.

The *Johnston* remained off Guam until August 8, screening a bombardment group until Ritidian and Pati Points were neutralized. Before the sun set on the eighth, Evans was halfway through preparing his report. At his typewriter that evening, he recorded his suggestions for future operations and the lessons learned from this one.

The liberation of Guam was an accomplishment that dramatically increased the quality of life for the island's residents. Nowhere yet had American liberators been received with more enthusiasm than on the islands of Guam and Saipan. Life there had been peaceful and idyllic in the early years of the war, but once the Americans began traveling on the road to Tokyo, the Japanese army immediately enforced martial law. "A number were executed for exhibiting 'American sympathy,' in forms such as looking up with a smile at an American plane," wrote historian Morison. The Japanese perpetrated on the local population "cruelties and sadism beyond the understanding of the average human mind," recalled a resident of Guam about the occupation.

Evans and his sailors had worked around the clock and been at the beck and call of Marines ashore for more than two weeks. They were ready whenever a flare was thrown up in desperation or a call for help went out on the TBS circuit. If the battle for Guam had lasted months, as it had on Guadalcanal, Evans would have been up to the task, and his crew would have followed him.

For Evans, Guam represented his greatest opportunity to appreciate how far he and his crew had come, but for the war effort, it meant something else. It represented the most significant step on the road to Tokyo. Soon the airfield would be reconstructed and expanded, allowing B-29 bombers with a range of just under six thousand miles to be based there. Tokyo is less than sixteen

hundred miles north of Guam, and the capture of this island reduced Japan's hope for winning the war.

Evans and his crew were licking their chops and reveling in the
work they had done as they left Guam and sailed for Eniwetok.
The next step for the Allies was the conquest of the Philippines.
More fighting lay ahead.

CHAPTER 9

Within Three Days of Being One Year Old

AUGUST 1944–OCTOBER 24, 1944

With Guam captured, Evans on August 9 brought his destroyer from there with the screen of Task Force 53, the force of battleships and cruisers that had bombarded Guam and was bound for Eniwetok Atoll in the Marshall Islands. Assured of his executive officer's ability to manage the ship, Evans spent much of the next forty-eight hours in his cabin typing his after-action report. With his Underwood typewriter, Evans put into writing his opinion of his ship's performance and drew attention to the standout performances of key officers.

More important, Evans worked to frame improvements for future operations. Fresh in Evans's memory were the anxieties caused by not knowing the exact location of troops ashore and the delay and confusion caused from using a shared fire support radio frequency. Evans asked, among his recommendations, that tanks carry on their rears fluorescent panels capable of illuminating them and providing clear lanes of fire to bombardment ships.

Evans also asked that tanks be fitted with radios, because they often traveled ahead of the soldiers and encountered enemy strongpoints earlier than ground units. All of this, Evans believed, would have made his job easier.

After-action reports were probably not all Evans wrote. During the second day of the trip to the Marshalls from Guam, Evans's crew passed sixty-three bags of mail to the cruiser *Louisville* to be sent stateside. Evans was on the bridge as his ship closed to within twenty yards, and sacks were exchanged by a system of ropes. In letters home Evans typically avoided the sentimental, writing largely to ask how mortgage payments were going and if his two boys were performing well in school.

Many crew members, however, gushed to their families about their sense of accomplishment. According to Bob Hagen, "[W]e knew by this time that we were the finest bombardment ship in the fleet." Evans knew their ship was not special among the hundreds of destroyers in theater, but he must have allowed himself personal pride particularly after the skill shown in the destruction of the position on Neye Island, where his crew had so skillfully rocked back and forth in the high tide.

In his cabin Evans forged his fourteen-page report, then placed it in a binder and signed each page, readying it for the force commander's staff. He finished before anchoring on the thirteenth of August in Eniwetok Lagoon. After anchoring, orders placing his ship on twenty-four hours' notice and attaching it to Task Unit 53.4.5 were brought to his cabin; that task unit was composed of three battleships, two heavy cruisers, and Destroyer Division 94. Evans likely scratched his head. Maybe the Palau Islands were next for bombardment, but he could not know. In any case the twenty-four-hours' notice meant that his crew would have time to relax aboard while at Eniwetok.

New orders did not come until after a relaxing week. On the morning of August 19, Evans addressed his crew over the intercom, appealing to their pride for their performance at Guam. He relayed that they were being sent south to Espiritu Santo, Vanuatu. There they could expect to greet several carriers that had just arrived from the United States.

His screws were already churning water when he set down the phone. The trip south was routine until before the morning general quarters drill on the twenty-third, the two old battleships *Tennessee* and *California* collided and forced the column to act with urgency. The *Tennessee*'s rudder jammed, heeling her into the *California* and tearing off part of the *California*'s bow. Evans reported to the bridge and ordered the *Johnston* to screen the stricken battlewagon, which had come to a halt. After several hours, the destroyer *Hailey* was detailed to stay behind and escort *California* as she limped away, freeing Evans to continue to Espiritu Santo, where the *Johnston* dropped anchor on the morning of August 24.

There, to his surprise, he saw only battleships and cruisers. The carriers it seemed had gone ahead to Guadalcanal. He left to join them on the afternoon of the twenty-seventh, reaching Purvis Bay on Florida Island two days later. There he took on fuel and received a few bags of letters that had been chasing them since they left Guam. Evans went on the intercom and told his crew that whether the men had received love letters from home or "Dear John" letters, they must wait until night to answer them. This day, they had work to do: sailing out to meet three escort carriers that were north of Guadalcanal and needed escort to Purvis Bay for fuel. This they accomplished by the morning of September 1, and there the *Johnston* remained at anchor until leaving again with the carriers on September 4.

Evans and his crew appreciated the time to rest, but it also allowed sailors to get into trouble drinking from stores of grain alcohol hidden underneath the sand and surf around Florida Island. Edward Block was older than most aboard and possessed the savvy to procure alcohol. Evans knew the younger sailors looked up to Block—and not just because he was a hard worker.

Before their operation with the three escort carriers, Evans had a list of awards to give to his sailors whose work had been exemplary. While reading over the list, Evans immediately recognized the opportunity for a joke. He ordered one of his junior officers to call Edward Block to his cabin before the evening GQ drill on the third; then Evans left to finish some paperwork in his cabin. Over the intercom came "Block, report to the captain!" The junior officer repeated his message twice before suddenly hanging up. Block thought, *What the hell have I done now?* As he walked toward the captain's wardroom, he considered for a moment that maybe the captain wanted another haircut, or else he was about to be chewed out for supplying alcohol to the crew.

Evans was in his cabin when he heard a knock on his door and Block's voice asking if he might enter. Evans pretended to consider the question before granting permission. Block came in with a sheepish grin on his face, asking if Evans needed another haircut. Evans shook his head no and turned to his desk, keeping silent as he sifted through papers.

He let Block sweat for a few moments before turning toward him and calmly saying, "Block, it is my pleasure to present you with the Good Conduct Ribbon." Evans stood up and walked toward the sailor until they were face-to-face. Then he said, "I don't know how you did it. I guess you just never got caught." Without responding Block saluted his captain and left, thinking on his way out, *You are right.*

The next morning, September 4, after all the awards had been handed out, the *Johnston* weighed anchor and sortied with the anti-submarine screen of the carriers *Kalinin Bay, Petrof Bay,* and *Saginaw Bay.* It took ten days for the *Johnston* to cover the twelve hundred miles to reach their new destination, Peleliu in the Palau Islands, an archipelago west of the Caroline Island group. The days at sea were marked by the comings of aircraft on the three carriers under its screen. Dozens of aircraft sorties were flown per day from the carriers, and once combat operations commenced off the islands, that number would increase. For this next mission, the *Johnston* would remain in one of the screening positions around the carriers.

When Evans arrived off Peleliu on Dog Day—the fifteenth of September—there were already dozens of LSTs waiting to carry the First Marine Division onto the coral beachhead. As at Guam the bombardment force lined up a mile from the beach, and the first wave of Marines made their approach on an orchestrated schedule. The *Johnston* was farther out to sea, not participating in the bombardment.

It was fierce. The island was only six miles wide and two long, but battleships pounded it with a rate of fire that would have sufficed for an island triple the size. This was thought more than adequate, for it was expected to be an easy landing. From the *Johnston*'s bridge, Evans watched the LSTs move toward the beach.

Adjacent to him on the bridge, charts of the island had been laid out, but he was not called in for fire support, which must have rankled after what his crew and he had shown at Guam.

Evans's anxiety, though, increased when pilots overhead reported Japanese troops rushing out from caves, unaffected except for being blinded by the equatorial sun. The initial surprise turned into a nightmare for both Marines and those offshore listening to fire support frequencies as they realized the Japanese had held thousands of troops in defensive caves.

Evans documented how his crew "listened intently to the progress of the landings over the air observer's circuit and enviously to the bombardments over the fire support common frequency. This was the first operation we have been in since commissioning that this ship had not been assigned to a close-in fire-support mission." He could do nothing except throw himself into his job.

Screening for carriers was a tedious task by nature, but the *Johnston*'s job off Peleliu was made worse by wind conditions. To actively hunt submarines, a ship needed to be traveling at around twelve to thirteen knots, but the *Johnston* needed to steam at twenty knots just to keep up with the movement of the carriers, each angling its flight deck to place it into the headwind. At high speeds it was impossible to use the *Johnston*'s submarine-finding sonar because of the interference of her own engine noise. "The screen was reorienting continuously at high speeds that practically no anti-submarine protection could possibly be given," Evans wrote.

This was the closest Evans ever got to complaining. He carried out his assignment faithfully as he listened to the progress of the invasion. The first day of fighting brought the Marines to the end of the airstrip on Peleliu's southwestern portion—what gave the island its importance—and after another three hard days, the Marines removed the Japanese from the airfield and pushed the defenders a half mile inland, to the foot of a rise of coral and rock named Umurbrogol Mountain.

This mountain was honeycombed with hundreds of interconnected limestone caves that housed thousands of Japanese soldiers. The island was easily visible to reconnaissance pilots, but for them to accurately describe it to Marines under fire was difficult because of the uniqueness of its terrain. On the ground the Marines fought blindly, often running into sinkholes, concealed bunkers, Japanese strongpoints, and indefensible positions without any warning.

The island had been expected to fall within a week, but after the Marines had been on Peleliu for five days, the fighting was still desperate. In the caves on Peleliu, Japanese defenders drank sake and prepared to sacrifice themselves.

It was tough for everyone aboard the *Johnston* to keep their minds off the Marines. If Evans had had his way, he would have taken his gig over to some captain or admiral and demanded ammunition, then brought his destroyer near shore and fired until his barrels glowed red. Evans was left stewing until the twentieth of September, when orders came for the escort carriers to withdraw from Peleliu.

On the morning of the twenty-first, Evans left with them and sailed two hundred miles east to the Ulithi Atoll, which had been taken by the Allies eight months earlier and served as a forward operating base. Ulithi's islands formed a vast lagoon of more than three hundred square miles of protected water. More ships could enter than at Pearl Harbor, and there the fleet waited to strike again.

On the evening of the twenty-fourth, the crew of the *Johnston* enjoyed a movie on the fantail. To Evans this must have felt like lazy Manila, but the next day the war found him again. On the morning of the twenty-fifth, he maneuvered his destroyer out of the atoll in pursuit of a submarine reported by air patrols. After the *Johnston* had dropped eighteen depth charges to no apparent effect, it was assumed that the contact had been an error.

Evans's heart quickly returned to its resting rate after he realized the contact was false, but there was little time to rest. At just past five in the afternoon, Evans sortied with a carrier force and started southeast, then covered a thousand miles to New Guinea. He was screening the escort carriers *Gambier Bay*, *Kitkun Bay*, and *White Plains*; this task unit arrived at Humboldt Bay, New Guinea, on the twenty-eighth and was placed on two-hour alert, then left the next afternoon for Manus Island in the Admiralty Island chain. When Evans pulled his ship into Seeadler Harbor—the anchorage west of Manus Island—on October 4, his mind raced for an answer to what was coming next, for dozens of ships lay at anchor here.

Their hint came on October 9. With the Marianas captured and the long-range threats in the Carolines and Palau neutralized, the fleet was ready to sink its teeth into the next operation: the long-awaited invasion of the Philippines. A secret dispatch was forwarded to ship captains of the Seventh Fleet, and when Evans took it in hand, his heart raced. The plan called for the Seventh Fleet to support landings by the Sixth Army on the central Philippine island of Leyte. No fewer than eighteen escort carriers from the Seventh Fleet were to be deployed east of Leyte and Samar, the next island to the north, in an area known as Leyte Gulf, and they would operate in three groups of six, each denoted the radio call signs Taffy 1, 2, and 3. Their aircraft would attack Japanese positions before boots hit the sand, and the carriers would remain to provide support as the Army moved inland.

Throughout the afternoon of October 10, Evans briefed his officers as they lay at anchor in Seeadler Harbor. During the operation, their destroyer, Evans explained, would be attached to the screen for Taffy 3, the northernmost of the carrier groups, positioned along the eastern mouth of Leyte Gulf. The three Taffy units would operate roughly fifty miles apart.

The escort carriers, also known as jeep carriers, had the hull designation CVE, which some jokers thought stood for "Combustible, Vulnerable, and Expendable." They had a less prestigious screening assignment, because their low speed and smaller air wing prevented them from being used aggressively, in the way that larger fleet carriers are used. As Evans briefed his men, Lieutenant Hagen expressed particularly loud grief about the assignment. His view, he explained, was that their performance at Guam should have merited a weightier task—instead of them being stuck with those "pestiferous flattops," he proclaimed. Evans silently agreed, though not in front of his men. Diplomatically, Evans told Hagen that this assignment was essential for the Army and that these operations there were critical to give America a staging ground for an invasion of Japan.

Evans had concerns, though, not about the strategic credibility of the mission at Leyte, but about his lack of ability now to fulfill the promise he had made to his crew almost a year earlier: that his would be a fighting ship. Evans held hope, though, that with the Third Fleet operating nearby, his destroyer might just be shuffled over to screen Admiral William "Bull" Halsey's battleships and large frontline fleet carriers. These Navy weapons were given free reign by Admiral Nimitz to hunt Japanese surface ships, Evans knew, and he wanted in on that action. But as he prepared to leave Seeadler Harbor, no new order came to detach from the Seventh Fleet and join Third Fleet.

In the predawn hours of the twelfth of October, the *Johnston* left Manus Island with Taffy 3 and Admiral Jesse Oldendorf's bombardment group of cruisers and battleships. To the crew, this was just another support mission, similar to their work off Peleliu. However, given their objective—the Philippine Islands, to which General Douglas MacArthur had vowed to return—Evans responded with extra urgency.

Many of Evans's sailors regarded this invasion as a publicity stunt for General MacArthur. Their feelings were understandable but wrong. Evans appreciated the Philippines as more than the islands from which MacArthur had been pushed in 1942. Evans had lived in Manila and spent weeks at sea refueling the submarines and the archaic destroyers of the prewar Asiatic Fleet. He knew the importance of the Philippines. Their protected harbors and sea-lanes and massive islands provided a gateway into the South China Sea.

En route to Leyte, on the sixteenth of October, Taffy 3 smacked headlong into a typhoon. It was unavoidable. The eye of the storm was moving westward along their path. The carriers turned southwest into the fifty-six-knot wind so they could retrieve their planes; then they turned back northwest before being broadsided by massive forty-foot waves. Taffy 3 aviators barely had time to return to their flight decks and have their aircraft tied down and their ballast tanks filled.

For the next twenty-four hours, Evans's destroyer pitched and rolled. The *Johnston* and the *Fletchers* were built to roll as much as fifty degrees and come back, but the sailors in her were not. Evans ordered his ship into Material Condition Baker; all hatches were sealed shut and the crew remained inside. In the crew quarters, poker games were interrupted by the pronounced click of the intercom as Evans picked up the PA phone. Enforcers like Clyde Burnett came rushing through, yelling, hitting men on the shoulders, and forcing them to stow their cards before waves began tossing them around.

On the bridge Evans labored to keep the ship heading into the enormous seas, and he looked out sharply to port and starboard, aware that a rogue wave or a massive confluence of two or more waves that towered up together could crash into them from any quarter. Evans's strength did not leave him for twenty-four hours as he stood at the helm maneuvering his ship. Once the danger was passed, he could smile that at least he had earned another sea story that he could tell his children once home.

Taffy 3 arrived off Leyte Island on October 18, two days ahead of the Sixth Army. For two days the pilots of Taffy 3 ruled the skies. When the Third Fleet arrived with the Sixth Army, the massive air wings on Admiral Halsey's fleet carriers now provided the most support. The three carrier groups of Third Fleet, commanded by Admiral Marc Mitscher under Halsey, assumed the responsibility of deterring any Japanese counterattack, while the Taffy 3 aviators would assist the Army efforts on Leyte and Samar.

Also with Halsey's Third Fleet were Admiral Willis Lee's modern battleships. They would spread out across the San Bernardino Strait, the most northern route east to west through the Philippines, to counter a Japanese counterattack from the sea.

It was almost certain that the Japanese would come from the San Bernardino Strait, if they came at all. Although narrow, twisting, difficult, and swept by an eight-knot current, the strait saved the ships from having to make an eight-hundred-mile trip to circle the northern edge of Luzon. Navy planners gave Admiral Lee's battleships the task of covering the seven-mile-wide exit to the strait.

On October 20, MacArthur sloshed ashore at Leyte with his accustomed self-satisfied ostentation, then posed for a picture with several young soldiers. Thousands of soldiers and hundreds of vehicles crossed the beaches, and Halsey's aviators, positioned over the horizon from Admiral Lee's battleships, swarmed the skies, giving General MacArthur the photogenic backdrop he desired for his iconic "I have returned" reappearance in the Philippines.

To the north, in Leyte Gulf, Evans sat aboard the *Johnston* watching the comings and goings of the Taffy 3 aircraft. On the one hand, he could have felt proud to have escorted the first carriers to reach Leyte Gulf, though his pride was still wounded that his ship had not been attached to Halsey. The Seventh Fleet's light, slow escort carriers had just been tools to serve General MacArthur's landing. It was an embarrassment shared by Evans's entire crew.

Together, the pilots of all the combined carrier groups spent five profitable days bombing, strafing, and firing rockets onto the

Japanese airfields and aviation facilities on Luzon and Leyte. Once the Third Fleet arrived, though, it was harder for Evans to remain diplomatic about his rear echelon assignment. Still, he had his orders, and his job for now was submarine deterrence. Dutifully, he studied charts of the ocean floor and speculated with his officers about where submarines might approach them. Evans did not believe that the Japanese would allow the Army landing to go unopposed, but with the presence of so many patrolling aircraft, he did not think that his submarine screening efforts were needed.

"Bull" Halsey was operating his carriers and battleships northeast of Samar. His unit, designated Task Force 38, had been deployed to block Japan's expected response to the Army landing on Leyte Island. Japanese naval forces were expected to travel directly through the Philippines west to east, exiting the Philippines' interior waters through the San Bernardino Strait. That Halsey was placed there to block them gave Evans what assurance he had that the *Johnston* might have a hand in a fight.

By the time of the landing on October 20, the *Johnston*'s Taffy 3 was off Samar, Taffy 2 was tracing circles in the sea forty miles to Evans's south, and Taffy 1 was eighty miles south of him. South of all three Taffy groups, Admiral Oldendorf's force of old battleships was covering the exit of the Surigao Strait, the other possible, though less likely, direction from which the Japanese might appear. If the Japanese were going to attack, either Admiral Halsey's new fast battleships or Oldendorf's lumbering old battlewagons, or both, were going to fight.

CHAPTER 10

Sho-Go

ADMIRAL KURITA'S DILEMMA

By the summer of 1944, it was clear to the Japanese that they would lose the war. However, many Japanese leaders believed that they would be able to keep some or all of their captured territory if they were able to force the Allies into negotiations before they secured victory. Accordingly a plan by the name of Sho-Go ("Victory Operation") was written.

Japanese intelligence did its work well. After the losses of Saipan and Guam, it seemed apparent that the next American assault would be on the Philippines proper, and that attack must be hurled back at all costs. In early July, all the available ships assembled at Lingga, Sumatra, where the battleships and cruisers were fitted with radar and every antiaircraft battery that could be found was mounted on the decks. Even seamen were trained with rifles to shoot at aircraft.

The principal commanders flew to Manila on August 10 and Sho-Go was presented to them. This plan called for the consolidation of the battleship-and-cruiser fleet into two groups and for a third group, formed of the remaining four carriers in the Imperial Navy, to be created. The target would be the American invasion on the Philippines, which intelligence had narrowed to three possible locations and which Japanese submarine captains and guerrilla operators said was moving forward. The two battleship forces would attack the American Army invasion beachhead from the south and north before the troops had a chance to firmly entrench themselves. The third group, the carriers, would sail down from Japanese coastal waters and become a diversionary unit intended to bait the American battleships away from the Army invasion beachhead and ultimately serve as a sacrifice.

It was accepted that the Japanese troops must destroy the American forces within two days of their landing or the objective would elude the Japanese, and it was accepted that while Sho-Go counted on air support from their planes on Luzon, such aid would likely not be effective and the ships would have to defend themselves from air attacks. Vice Admiral Takeo Kurita was named to command the strongest unit, the Center Force. He and his chief of staff, Rear Admiral Tomiji Koyanagi, and the other commanders were horrified. To take such extreme risks—in confined waters, with hopelessly complicated communications, with little or no air cover, and for no greater objectives than shooting up empty transports and bombarding troops already ashore—was nonsense. Victory lay in destroying the growing power of the American carriers and dispatching American capital ships in a fleet surface action. But, as Koyanagi wrote later, the orders came from Combined Fleet's commander in chief, Admiral Soemu Toyoda, and he was not to be questioned.

Combined Fleet knew that the plan was a gamble, but if the northern force succeeded as a decoy and pulled away Halsey's fleet carriers and new sixteen-inch gun battleships from the eastern exit of the San Bernardino Strait, the American gambit in the Philippines could be wrecked, and their timetable could be set back by months. By then Japan's gigantic new aircraft carrier, *Shinano*, could join the war, new pilots could be trained, and time could buy other benefits.

Japanese reconnaissance confirmed what captured pilots had told them: Admiral Halsey's powerful Third Fleet was positioned at the entrance of the San Bernardino Strait, from which Kurita, as commander of the Center Force, would have to emerge to attack the American landings. If Halsey were removed from the San Bernardino Strait, the Center Force would move through it, cut south, then attack the Army on the beach. However, Japanese reconnaissance had not learned that there were three escort carrier groups also positioned north of the beachhead. The southernmost of Japanese naval forces in the Sho-Go plan would attempt to sneak through the Surigao Strait on the twenty-third of October, then move north and attack the Army beachhead on Leyte from the south. In Tokyo, Admiral Jisaburo Ozawa boarded his flagship, the carrier *Zuikaku*, and in league with three lighter carriers and a screen of escorts bore south, moving slowly and lazily through American submarine routes, hoping to be spotted.

———

In command of the Center Force, Kurita was the one most tasked with the destruction of the American beachhead. He was one of the Imperial Navy's most experienced, most battle-tested, and most controversial officers. He was also the one who would find himself the most bedeviled and embattled by the American destroyer captain Ernest Evans. Kurita was fifty-five, and ironically, he had spent more of his career commanding destroyers, and five different destroyer divisions, than performing any other duty. No other officer in the Imperial Navy understood destroyers, their uses, their possibilities, and their limitations better than he. In one of history's exquisite juxtapositions, he was the perfect foil for Evans.

To prepare for the attack, the entire Japanese battle fleet advanced from Lingga to Borneo, their closest anchorage to the Philippines. When they learned that the Americans had landed in force on the eastern shore of Leyte Island on the morning of October 20, 1944, Sho-Go was triggered. The Southern Force under Admiral Shoji Nishimura, flying his pennant from the battleship *Yamashiro* and accompanied by her sister, *Fuso*, stood out from Borneo in company with the heavy cruiser *Mogami* and four destroyers. Kurita was confident that Nishimura could take care of himself; what worried him was the part to be played by his good friend Jisaburo Ozawa. Why had his powerful fleet carrier *Zuikaku* been reduced to the role of a decoy to lure Halsey away from the main action?

The answer was, the Japanese naval air arm had already been decimated. All six of their fleet carriers had participated in the attack on Pearl Harbor, and now *Zuikaku* was the lone survivor. Four had been lost at Midway, and *Zuikaku*'s sister, *Shokaku*, had been sunk in the Battle of the Philippine Sea four months earlier, along with the one other large Japanese carrier, *Taiho*. As few carriers as were left, there were fewer airplanes and still fewer pilots. Japan, as a naval airpower, was already finished, which meant that sooner or later, the Imperial Navy would be finished. On December 7, 1941, the Japanese had demonstrated that airplanes could sink anchored battleships when they shattered the American Pacific Fleet at Pearl Harbor. Three days later they proved that airplanes could sink battleships maneuvering in the open by sending HMS *Repulse* and HMS *Prince of Wales* to the bottom of the South China Sea.

And now, pondered Kurita, his powerful force of twenty-three vessels—including five battleships, among them the two most powerful on earth, *Yamato* and *Musashi*—was being sent into confined waters with virtually no air cover. The talk had already begun that Operation Sho-Go was a glorious suicide mission. Kurita had a long-earned reputation as a steady and reliable officer: He did his job, he obeyed orders, and he never made excuses. He was the perfect fall guy to lead an impossible mission. The greatest criticism of Kurita was that he lacked zeal for the cult of the emperor; another was that he was a cautious commander, not a risk-taker. Some of the men thought it cowardly that he hoisted his pennant in the heavy cruiser *Atago* when he might have chosen the overpowering *Yamato*. The lowly seamen were unaware that this order had come straight from Combined Fleet General Staff. They expected the campaign to open with a night action, which was traditionally spearheaded by heavy cruisers.

This order likely sat well with Kurita, for the additional reason of his distaste for *Yamato*'s commander, Admiral Matome Ugaki, a political zealot who constantly praised the goal of dying for the emperor. Ugaki had been chief of staff to Admiral Isoroku Yamamoto, the architect of the Pearl Harbor attack and commander in chief at the time of his death. Yamamoto and Kurita, however, were of the same mind regarding vainglory: that wasting lives to make useless sacrifices was pointless and foolish.

When it came down to it, could Kurita be counted on to lead his task force into mass suicide, and for what? It was apparent now that once the operation was triggered, he could not possibly reach the landing zone until the American troops had been ashore for five days. Even if he succeeded in getting there, he would be able to sink nothing but empty transports. There can be little doubt that he resented his orders to head his ships northeast up the Palawan Passage and open his part of the attack.

As a matter of navigation, the first few hundred miles were the easiest: to sortie from Brunei and steam northeast along the long, skinny line of the Philippine island of Palawan, not straying too far from it so as to avoid the shoals in the South China Sea.

It did not go well. On the night of October 22–23, the American submarines *Darter* and *Dace*, patrolling this Palawan Passage, saw Kurita's ships coming and raced to get in position to attack. As the fleet passed, *Darter* fired four torpedoes into Kurita's own *Atago*. She capsized and sank in eighteen minutes, leaving the admiral to be rescued as he swam away from her; he transferred his flag to Ugaki's *Yamato*. *Dace* sank the heavy cruiser *Maya*, and *Darter* damaged the heavy cruiser *Takao* so severely that she was effectively put out of the war.

The submarines then independently hunted the stragglers, but when the *Darter* grounded on the night of October 24, the skipper of the *Dace* gave up the hunt, opting to pull his comrade off the coral before low tide left him vulnerable to attack by the wounded *Takao*.

With three heavy cruisers gone, Admiral Kurita forged ahead, aware that now his presence was known and that a more aggressive and overwhelming attack must have been imminent. The interior waters of the Philippines, with their seven thousand islands and rocks, are one of the earth's navigational nightmares. After the Palawan Passage, the fleet turned ninety degrees, to head southeast, then in a long loop back to the northeast to get around the south end of Mindoro Island and emerge into the island-strewn Sibuyan Sea. As they did so, at 1030 on the twenty-fourth, the American response came. Hundreds of aviators from Halsey's fast carriers swarmed, diving from nineteen thousand feet. The concerted humming of the Curtiss Helldivers' and Grumman Avengers' Wright Cyclone engines filled the air.

Ernest Evans was three hundred miles away in the Philippine Sea when a subordinate on Kurita's staff pointed toward the aircraft diving on the horizon, and then another lookout brought the admiral's attention to the torpedo bombers that were creeping toward them, sustaining level paths a mere eighty feet above the waves.

In defiance, Admiral Kurita ordered his secondary battery of five-inch and six-inch guns to open fire and create a field of flak that the dive-bombers would have to fly through twice: once on the way down, then on the way back up after releasing their bombs fifteen hundred feet above the targets. The Japanese sailors had fallen under the thrall of their colossal super battleships and believed they were invulnerable. They also eagerly believed the propaganda they had been told that American pilots were sissies and cowards. Great was their shock as they saw American pilots fly unswervingly into the teeth of more than a hundred antiaircraft guns, and sometimes through the ships' very rigging, to release their ordnance. And they watched in tears and horror, dumbfounded, as the attack concentrated on their beloved *Musashi* and overwhelmed her with a combined thirty-five bombs and torpedoes. She went dead in the water, down by the head and listing.

Watching from the *Yamato*, which had herself absorbed a pair of five-hundred-pound bombs that struck near the forward turrets and cut her speed, Kurita estimated his chances of survival. From the number of attacking aircraft, more than two hundred forty, the admiral surmised that they could only have come from the large carriers with Halsey's Third Fleet, which meant that a line of his new sixteen-inch-gun battleships was with him also. If Kurita pressed forward, he would face more air attacks—his men had endured five this day—in addition to the large guns of the American battle fleet. Unable to retaliate against the American carriers, Admiral Kurita turned his force around and retired back to the west.

It was a victory for the Third Fleet. However, ego bled through in the after-action reporting. The pilots, detailing their attack, mentioned that dozens of torpedo and bomb hits were made on multiple Japanese ships. This was true, but the pilots failed to mention that more than ninety percent of the blows had landed on a single battleship, the doomed *Musashi*. Yes, the Japanese had retreated back to the west, but Admiral Kurita's fleet had not been destroyed. By 1715 on the twenty-fourth, with repairs made, fleet speed restored, and, above all, the lack of further American air attacks suggesting that Halsey might have broken off to go chasing after Ozawa, Kurita turned his Center Force back east. Kurita's conjecture was prophetic, for on the afternoon of the twenty-fourth, Third Fleet aircraft on patrol sighted Ozawa's four Japanese decoy carriers two hundred miles to the north. Before nightfall Halsey, believing that Kurita was retreating, took the bait, deserted the San Bernardino Strait, and charged after his new prey.

In the predawn hours of October 25, the Center Force completed its delicate threading of the San Bernardino Strait after battling the eight-knot current. The only way to get through had been to steam ahead in a single line, with the fleet stretching more than ten miles. That they made the passage at night without incident was a triumph of skilled navigation.

They emerged from the strait into the broad open waters of the Philippine Sea, with Halsey nowhere to be seen, and Kurita splayed his fleet out in battle formation across several square miles of ocean. He had lost three heavy cruisers in the Palawan Passage, and the seventy-two-thousand-ton *Musashi*, once thought invulnerable, now lay at the bottom of the Sibuyan Sea. Kurita, however, still commanded a force of withering power and, more than that, one that epitomized the very rise of Japanese naval power in the twentieth century.

His oldest battleship was the IJN *Kongo*, laid down in 1911 and British built by Vickers in Barrow-in-Furness. The ship, designed as a battle cruiser, sacrificed armor for speed and mounted a battleship's eight fourteen-inch guns. The conceptual flaws of the battle cruiser had been laid bare at the Battle of Jutland in 1916, when HMS *Invincible, Queen Mary,* and *Princess Royal* all blew up (prompting Admiral Beatty's famous remark, "There seems to be something wrong with our bloody ships today."). The Japanese took note, and, once back home, they gave *Kongo* a thorough rebuilding, adding several thousand tons of armor and improved engineering that actually increased her speed. Nobody expected the lightly regarded Japanese to create the world's first fast battleship, a new designation that rendered every previous battleship in every other nation's navy obsolete and forced them to begin catching up.

Kurita's second battleship, IJN *Haruna*, was *Kongo's* sister, younger by fourteen months and built by the Japanese as they gained their own shipbuilding capabilities. Like *Kongo* she was converted to a fast battleship with increased speed and armor. The third, IJN *Nagato*, commissioned in 1920, was half a generation newer and the only imperial battleship with sixteen-inch guns installed to match the American *Colorados*. She had taken two bomb hits in the Sibuyan Sea but was once more operational.

Japan had been a British and American ally in World War I, but getting short shrift at the Washington Naval Conference in 1921 had been a deeply felt insult and Japan had ended its participation with those countries in 1936. As battleship design entered a third generation, and the U.S. settled on a standard armament of three triple turrets of sixteen-inch guns and the new British design mounted ten fourteen-inch guns, the Japanese answered by building two monster battleships of stupefying power. *Yamato* and *Musashi* mounted three triple turrets of 18.1-inch guns, with speed and armor as well to overshadow anything that the British or Americans had even imagined. *Musashi* was gone, but *Yamato* plowed into the Philippine Sea flying the admiral's pennant.

Of Kurita's six heavy cruisers, the first three in line—*Kumano*, *Suzuya*, and *Chikuma*—were the most powerful of their kind in the world. They were not new. They had been announced under the restrictions of the Washington treaty as light cruisers. But at a full load of eleven thousand tons, they were by far the largest light cruisers ever built, and they mounted no fewer than five triple turrets of six-inch guns. What had not been announced was that the barbettes for those cruisers had been designed to pull out the triple six-inch turrets and replace them with double eight-inch turrets when Japan was ready to throw over the treaty. That replacement would give the vessels more eight-inch guns with more throw weight of high-explosive shells than on the Allies' counterparts, except for the American *Pensacolas*.

Once in open water, Kurita turned south and went down the eastern shore of Samar Island, bound for those American landings on Leyte. In Kurita's mind, he was still on a fool's errand that had already proved costly, but morning was not far gone when his lookouts sighted something almost too good to be true: Far to their south on the horizon, the silhouettes of six American aircraft carriers could just be seen. From that distance, Kurita believed that they were *Essex*-class fleet carriers and that Halsey and his battle fleet were by then far to the north. Perhaps Toyoda had been right; perhaps the gamble would be worth it. The prospect was enough to get even Kurita's cynical blood up, and the signal flags were hoisted: general attack.

———

In the predawn of that same morning, Ernest Evans, sleeping in his cabin aboard the *Johnston*, was awakened suddenly by the flashes and crumping booms of distant gunfire coming not from the north but from the south.

After the war Lieutenant Hagen recalled a conversation that he had had with Commander Evans on the night of October 24. The two men were standing on the fantail, lamenting their lack of combat. The ocean passed by at fifteen knots. The bubbling of the water in their wake drowned out their conversation.

"Well," Evans declared, almost biting his tongue, "we're within three days of being one year old. It's been an uneventful year." At this, Hagen scoffed, because "we'd only been through four invasions, but, since we hadn't even a flake of paint knocked off us or a man killed by an enemy shell, it was 'uneventful.'" After a moment of silence, Hagen conceded, "How are we ever going to keep our shooting hand in, playing nursemaid to plane-toting tubs?" Then Hagen took another drag from his cigarette, exhaled, and added, "[W]hat was the matter with the Admiral [Kinkaid] anyhow? Didn't he know what we had done at Guam?"

Hagen wrote later, "The skipper was a fighting man from the soles of his broad feet to the ends of his straight black hair." His attitude was that he had somehow let his crew down. Hagen felt that Evans held on to hopes that they would be attached to Halsey's Third Fleet carriers, and Halsey had a nose for where the action was. The need, however, was to the contrary. The workload placed on the Seventh Fleet escort carriers was going to continue to be heavy, and it was not expected to decrease for three more weeks at least as Army engineers labored to clear enough airfields on Leyte. Until Army pilots could assume their own air support, the escort carriers must bear the responsibility and the *Johnston* was needed to protect them.

They also talked about their next resupply and the availability of oil and ammunition. Although *Johnston* had drunk heavily from one of the Seventh Fleet tankers a few days earlier, their stores were low again. It had also been days since they last received ammunition. The Third Fleet received the reserves of armor-piercing shells; the escorts in the Seventh Fleet such as *Johnston* were an afterthought. The last ammunition resupply had brought on board only two hundred armor-piercing rounds for their five-inch guns. The rest of the nearly three thousand rounds Evans had stored in the magazines were proximity triggered, so they exploded in midair and were meant to hunt planes. Air defense was to be their only mission; Evans would not participate in the shore bombardment, and the thinking was that no surface attack was expected.

The day before, Evans had agreed to let one of his sailors—Clint Carter—shadow the radar division. The impressive capabilities of the new radar technology were lost on those who did not know about them or care to understand them. Some officers used the technology to keep their coffee warm; those more aware used it to score kills with naval rifles from eight miles away. The ships that had it gained vastly improved accuracy in gunfire, even at night. Every new *Fletcher*-class destroyer was equipped with it.

Carter was the gun captain at the number five five-inch mount, gun 55, but he felt that it would be "better with war's end to know more electrical and radar principles rather than just an ordnance repair." He and a radar officer chatted into the late hours of October 24 "of our wants and wishes for the future," Carter said. After waking up early on October 25, Carter got his introduction to the new technology by observing over the shoulders of the radarmen on morning watch.

Then, however, sailors from the radio room just above them came to alert the men in the CIC that a battle was being received on the radio. Carter was allowed to go up to the radio room to listen to it, and Evans, whose cabin was just across from the CIC, was also awakened. Through the chatter, Carter, Evans, and the radio operators could hear the torpedo boat captains as they confirmed putting their fish in the water, and the voices of gunnery officers broke through, celebrating direct hits on Japanese cruisers and battleships. The men of Taffy 3 on watch this night could clearly see what they thought was lightning on the horizon. Lookouts aboard the *Johnston* also reported seeing a storm, but soon word came from the radio shack to tell them that it was not lightning but the muzzle blasts of an almighty sea battle some eighty miles away.

What they were listening to on the radio and seeing lit on the horizon was the Battle of Surigao Strait and the annihilation of the Japanese Southern Force. True to the plan, Admiral Nishimura had approached the Leyte landing zone from his southerly route, but he was intercepted by Admiral Oldendorf and his squadron of six old battleships. Five of them—*Pennsylvania, Maryland, West Virginia, Tennessee,* and *California*—were ghosts that had been raised from the bottom of Pearl Harbor, and now they wreaked some vengeance. By the time the Japanese knew they were there, Oldendorf had already crossed their T—the ultimate position in naval warfare of bringing full broadsides to bear when the approaching enemy can reply only with the forward guns of the leading ship. Oldendorf's old battlewagons had also been fitted with radar gun control, so Nishimura never had a chance. He was killed when *Yamashiro* went down; *Fuso* with her beetling pagoda mast was sunk, as were the heavy cruiser *Mogami* and three destroyers, sent to the bottom either by Oldendorf's broadsides or by PT boats vectored in by his own *Fletcher*-class destroyers.

After the cries for a cease-fire went across the radio waves, Evans went to sleep and Carter returned to the radar with the goal of finishing his watch at 0400. For the rest of this watch, Carter practiced with the short-range radar equipment. It had a range of fifty miles, so each ship in Taffy 3 was visible. "The radar scope showed all the ships in our group," Carter recalled. Then, shortly before 0400, something happened. "Strange blips appeared on the outer fringe of the scope," remembered Carter. It was clearly a fleet fifty miles away. "Very shortly the Captain appeared, observed, and studied the problem for a few minutes as the range was closing." Evans did not believe that Halsey's fleet was still so close, so he made his way to the radio shack and had his men hail Admiral Clifton Sprague, the commander of Taffy 3.

Breaking the standing order for radio silence, Evans tuned in to the frequency for the carrier *Fanshaw Bay*. A member of Admiral Sprague's staff picked up. Then the admiral came on the radio and "proceeded to chew Captain Evans out because he had broken radio silence and declared he would pay the price for not following orders. He then informed the Captain the bogies we were tracking were the U.S. Third Fleet and to get the hell off the air," recalled Clint Carter. Evans was defeated, so he went back to sleep, leaving Carter to finish his first and final shift with the fire control radar.

CHAPTER 11

"Units of the Enemy Fleet Are Fifteen Miles Astern"

OCTOBER 25, 1944, 0530–0743

It was an ordinary morning that followed an abnormal night. Most sailors of Taffy 3 already knew that Admiral Halsey's pilots had beaten back Japanese warships as they approached the San Bernardino Strait. That became known as the Battle of the Sibuyan Sea. The action in the Surigao Strait was less known, but when the sailors woke up for general quarters drill at 0600, the word spread. However, general quarters would not be called for another hour.

The engines of the TBM Avengers were barely cold aboard the USS *Saint Lo* when at 0530 they started again. These pilots were going on routine patrol. They were jealous of what Halsey's aviators had gotten to do the day before.

Halsey's pilots had deflected the Center Force of Japan's Sho-Go plan. The counterattack on MacArthur's Philippine invasion appeared to have failed. The attempt by the Japanese Southern Force to break through the Surigao Strait had been blunted and the air attack in the Sibuyan Sea was successful; eighteen torpedoes and seventeen bombs had hit and crippled the battleship *Musashi*, leaving her to slip beneath the waves the next day. Accurate details on the air attack, though, were sparse. The leadership, including Halsey himself, heard that dozens of bomb and torpedo hits had been made. This same leadership failed to appreciate, however, that the hits were largely on the same target. The Center Force still deployed four powerful battleships, and after Halsey turned north after Ozawa's diversion force, there were no aviators who could stop them.

At 0530 the Grumman Avengers from VC-65 were making another anti-submarine patrol. Ten minutes later, at 0540, eight pilots from the 68th Fighter Squadron rose from the deck of the USS *Fanshaw Bay*, Taffy 3's flagship. They were prepared for dogfighting and ground support; beyond their service ammunition, they carried only light rockets and small bombs.

October 25 promised action, but not for the surface forces of Taffy 3. The Japanese submarine force was weak and the American bombers on patrol meant to keep it away, and the only credible surface threats had been repelled in the Battles of the Sibuyan Sea and Surigao Strait. It seemed that the *Johnston* was safe.

This morning Taffy 3 carriers moved southeast at fifteen knots. The wind was coming from the east, so a shift in this direction was needed to begin the day's flights. Sweeping over the deck, the wind opposed all forward progress and gave the aircraft engines greater torque at low power. The wind had been blowing from this direction for days. Enlisted sailors in berths near the port bow—the unit sailed northeast when not conducting flight operations—knew to expect the turning sensation whenever aircraft engines came alive above them each morning. It was one of many Pavlovian triggers aboard a ship, similar to the smell of breakfast in the mess or the sound of the Klaxon that sent sailors running to the ladders and doorways that took them to their battle stations. Every time aircraft engines started up, carrier sailors knew the ship would turn toward the wind.

The whole formation moved together. The destroyers and destroyer escorts loosely clung to the edge, forming a jagged array around the circle of carriers. The *Johnston* took the westernmost sector, one thousand yards southwest of the USS *White Plains*.

Evans had been asleep since waking up to assess the sonar contacts on the short-range radar shortly before 0400. However, the sailors on morning watch were up to see the morning patrol aircraft takeoff at 0540. Six minutes later the carriers made a pointed forty-five-degree turn back to the northeast to resume their patrol. The aircraft launched by the CVE's USS *Saint Lo* and *Fanshaw Bay* this morning were not meant to land for another couple of hours.

The carrier's path was divergent from Samar Island's coast. However, Taffy 3 needed to be within range of the Sixth Army's front lines, so later in the day, a new heading change to the south was needed. Until then, though, they would head northeast. When it was time to recover their aircraft, they would turn back into the easterly wind to do so.

When the *Johnston* held its morning general quarters drill, all aviators who would patrol this morning had been launched. It was lucky that the pilots would not need to land anytime soon, because shortly after the formation turned northeast, it sailed into some rain squalls. The *Johnston* remained west of the formation as they approached the rain.

Evans awoke at about 0615. Perhaps he woke up because of the sound of rain striking the lightly plated decking outside his cabin or perhaps because of the change of air pressure. Perhaps it wasn't noise or pressure that awoke Evans, but a feeling that this would be an abnormal day following the night when so much death had occurred in the Surigao Strait to the south.

Unable to sleep, Evans left his main cabin at 0615 and stuck his head into the CIC across the passageway to check in with those sailors. With Lieutenant Stirling in charge, they were drinking coffee and gave a quick acknowledgment to their captain. Since his men had nothing to report after the mystery radar sighting at 0400, Evans climbed the two decks up to the bridge.

Today, the sun was rising on his nearly two thousandth day at sea. He still had vastly more time at sea than anybody else aboard, but now the collective experience of war had seasoned his crew. Perhaps the collective abundance of combat experience aboard made Evans less of an enigma to his men, but none of his sailors had quite figured him out.

The sailors standing watch in the pilothouse and on the open bridge wings remembered after the war that Evans was up early. Two sailors on the bridge turned from their station and gave quick salutes. One sailor was manning the helm, one the power control lever, the helmsman and lee helmsman, respectively. Outside two other sailors were on watch. They did not mind their captain. Instead, they kept their eyes trained on the horizon. Evans then sat in his captain's chair and watched the sunrise.

The exaggerated rocking motion on the bridge could have tempted Evans to fall asleep in his captain's chair, but he was needed soon. After twenty minutes of sitting and gazing out at the predawn ocean, Evans ordered the officer on watch, Lieutenant Welch, to sound the Klaxon on the public address to signal battle stations. Morning general quarters was necessary because submarines often attack at dawn when the sun illuminates a ship on the water. The general quarters drill lasted only five minutes; then sailors relaxed their fighting stance and either returned to bed or went to the mess for coffee and an early breakfast.

This left Evans to descend the two ladders to his own cabin and enjoy a breakfast prepared by his Filipino steward. Ordinarily there would not be another drill until the afternoon. In his main cabin Evans enjoyed his breakfast and probably read from previous action reports, his favorite novel, or letters from home. His boys, now old enough to write, had likely penned him letters that were among the items he cherished in his private hours. They were not an emotional family, but his children certainly did write if only to show him that they could. Margaret certainly wrote to him, too, though only to talk about trivial things that would keep their house in order.

After the short breakfast and five or so minutes to himself, Evans aimed to return to his sea cabin at about 0630, stopping first at the CIC and then the radio room one level above. Hours earlier he had been listening to the drama of a battleship-versus-battleship duel, a rarity in the Pacific War, but now the radio room was silent, so he quickly returned to the bridge to see that all was in order. Then he made himself comfortable in his sea cabin.

In the pair of TBM Avengers launched off the USS *Saint Lo* this morning was that of Ensign William C. Brooks. He drew the sector to the north of Taffy 3 and was well clear of the *Johnston* when the first interaction with the enemy occurred this morning. His

gunner in the ball turret underneath him and his radioman behind him were both witnesses to the sudden and fateful encounter
with the Japanese battle fleet.

The *Johnston* had just secured from general quarters when
Ensign Brooks, flying north, peered down through a hole in the 7/10
cloud cover and spotted dozens of white wakes. Curious, the pilot
began scanning for the warships that had produced them. Brooks
had taken the ship recognition course, but at eighty-five hundred
feet, he could not make out those ships' nationality. Unsure if this
wasn't just Admiral Halsey's fleet, Brooks dove a thousand feet.

It was a beautiful but terrible sight: tapered pagoda masts, two
dozen of them, each towering over the midsection of its ship,
marking them as unmistakably Japanese.

In the cockpit Brooks's heart skipped a beat when he realized
his split second to react was over. Antiaircraft fire began pouring
from the guns of the large battleships and cruisers. The flak
touched his wings and the explosions rocked his fuselage. Brooks
pulled up, and as he did, he grabbed his microphone so that he
could raise the *Fanshaw Bay*.

The officer on duty in air plot aboard that carrier was stunned
to hear about a sighting of some two dozen Japanese ships twenty-
five miles to the north. Rear Admiral Clifton Sprague was promptly
informed. Waiting for a response Brooks circled the Japanese and
through the clouds stole glances at them, now out of reach. In a
matter of minutes, however, the battleships would close range on
Taffy 3, Brooks knew. They would assert themselves from nearly
twenty miles, and the gap would close in under twenty minutes.
The Japanese were coming from the northwest, almost west by
northwest at twenty knots, while Taffy 3 moved northeast at fifteen.

Brooks could not wait idly. He carried a load of depth charges and was assessing his options for attack when Admiral Sprague's voice came through the radio. Sprague laced into the aviator with a string of obscenities. He believed Brooks's report to be the work of a jumpy ensign. The sighting must have been Halsey's Third Fleet, Sprague estimated. The admiral was wrong, both in his judgment of the pilot's character and about the identity of the sighted fleet. Sprague realized his error almost immediately after stepping away from the radio. At 0642 lookouts on the *Fanshaw Bay* reported to Admiral Sprague the sighting of antiaircraft fire over the northern horizon, confirming what the young Avenger pilot had reported. Sprague regretted his actions at once.

Irritated, Brooks had descended to get a closer look, and as he did, black puffs of antiaircraft fire began buffeting his Avenger, but he would not pull up before descending to five thousand feet and delivering his three depth charges alongside a cruiser. This gesture was merely symbolic. The Japanese force continued toward Taffy 3 at twenty knots, soon twenty-five.

In the Japanese armada was the most powerful battleship ever built, *Yamato*, which alone at seventh-two thousand tons was almost twenty-seven times the weight of the *Johnston*. In fact she displaced more than all thirteen ships of Taffy 3. Recognizing the terrible mismatch that was developing, Sprague ordered his circular formation of CVEs to turn east into the wind, launch their aircraft, and make flank speed toward the cluster of rain squalls that offered concealment. Sprague's carriers needed to empty their flight decks of the flammable aircraft, with their fuel and their munitions.

Hundreds of personnel began running across the six flight

decks of Taffy 3. There was not enough time to arm the planes with the more explosive, and useful, weapons, such as five-hundred- and two-hundred-fifty-pound bombs. The planes were rushed off the deck, loaded with antipersonnel weapons for that day's mission. Rockets and light hundred-pound fragmentation bombs would be all they would have against the battleships of Admiral Kurita's Center Force. Even more futile were the aircraft equipped for anti-submarine patrol that carried only depth charges. No time was taken to rearm these aircraft. Every inch of the flight deck was roaring with the sounds of busy men at work laboring to get the explosives-laden aircraft off their ships before an enemy shell caused a massive explosion and subsequent blazing chain reaction.

Hoping to sink the American carriers before all of their planes were airborne, Admiral Kurita turned east by southeast. He later wrote that he had intended "to cripple the carriers' ability to have planes take off and land, and then to mow down the entire task force."

———

Evans was in his sea cabin when his lookouts spotted the antiaircraft fire. Aboard the *Fanshaw Bay*, Admiral Sprague was aware of the danger that his task force was in, but he had not yet given any reactive order nor had he addressed his captains. The individual ship captains of Taffy 3 ships watched as a layer of low-hanging charcoal lined the distant sky. Only after a momentary pause was it clear that this was antiaircraft fire rather than a rainstorm.

A series of shouts and a fusillade of rapid knocks to Evans's sea cabin door pulled him into the moment. It was a terrifying new reality. Below the horizon, beyond the earth's curve, an enemy was coming.

Reflexively Evans laced his boots and grabbed his battle helmet. Then he took a deep breath, steeling himself for the address he would make to his crew once he exited his sea cabin and stepped onto the bridge. The shells impacting the ocean sounded like a whale that had jumped from the sea, but then the delayed echo reached the crew, introducing the flying naval shells with sounds similar to those of passing freight trains. Belowdecks, sailors standing in line for breakfast dropped their trays and crossed the galley for the ladders that would bring them to their battle stations. Above them all, Evans, wearing his starched khaki uniform, stepped for the exit to his small sea cabin. Just four steps brought Evans to the bridge and his first action was to turn to the talk box to his right.

Eyes darted in his direction but were soon grabbed by the fifty-meter-tall towers of water rising near the carriers *White Plains* and *Fanshaw Bay*. Over Evans's shoulder, lookouts on the starboard bridge wing were looking up but Evans already knew aircraft were not their tormentors. These had to be the blips on the radar that Admiral Sprague had confused for Admiral Halsey earlier that morning.

In his PA address, Evans spoke directly to his crew, declaring that "units of the enemy fleet are fifteen miles astern. This is no drill! We are being pursued by a large portion of the Japanese Fleet." Then he slammed the phone down and turned to his next task.

Evans ordered his lee helmsman, "All ahead flank." In response the engine rooms raised steam and increased pressure inside each of the four air-encased boilers to 600 psi, powering the two propellers with a collective 60,000 shaft horsepower. The ship picked up pace quickly to her designated speed of thirty-eight knots.

From the bridge Evans watched as his crew scrambled onto the deck and then into the forward five-inch guns with the precision gained from their repeatedly practiced drills. They were orderly even with an enemy on the horizon. Pagoda masts were visible, but the ships' hulls were down below the waves. Their guns were underneath the horizon, too, but their spotter nests were high and Japanese gunners, excellent at the mathematics necessary for long-range fighting, were accurate. The U.S. carriers were their targets.

The specters of the Java Sea were coming back to haunt Evans. Within ninety seconds men took station at their antiaircraft guns, torpedo tubes, damage control positions, or main gun mounts, prepared to defend not only themselves but the carriers under their escort. The formation was heading northeast at the time that Evans ordered all ahead flank speed. He reacted quicker than the carriers and the admiral in charge of them. He was about to take the fight into his own hands. Evans knew to attack, regardless if he was ordered to or not.

Several moments after ordering up flank speed, Evans barked, "Left full rudder," to his helmsman. The helmsman quickly swung the destroyer to port and began heading northwest on a direct course toward the Japanese, moving underneath the arc of their shells. With this port turn to the northwest, Evans seized the tactical freedom that had evaded his captain in the Battle of the Java Sea. Then, the *Alden* had remained at the rear of the Allies' formation and waited for word to attack. Now, the *Johnston* did not.

Next Evans moved toward his helmsman, preparing to take the wheel himself. As he moved, Evans ordered an enlisted man to call the engine room. Taffy 3 needed a smoke screen. This was a cardinal duty of destroyers in the event of a surface fight. However, the sailors in the engine room were not used to hearing this order. They did not understand why they would risk highlighting their position to the Japanese. They had been trained to provide protection from attacking submarines, not surface ships.

Mechanic Charles Landreth picked up the phone in the engine room, and was surprised to hear an order to make smoke. "But we're not making smoke," the response came. "Up to this time they were always catching hell for making smoke," Landreth later admitted. The order was not followed. Irritated, Evans took the phone. "I want a smoke screen and I want it now," Evans demanded. A couple moments later, black funnel smoke began pouring from the *Johnston*'s two stacks. Then Evans picked the phone back up to address the crew again. "This is no drill," he quickly got out.

The small escort carriers could not outrun the Japanese force, and the Japanese shooting was becoming accurate. Though no hits were recorded in the opening minutes, a near miss on the carrier *White Plains* ruptured some hull plating and caused flooding below the waterline.

After Evans set down the phone, he looked into the passageway behind the bridge and saw Bob Hagen looking ferocious, ready for a fight. Hagen stood in the space beneath the gun director, waiting until the range had closed and the four other officers that worked with him had manned their positions in that metal box. "We were at 35,000 yards and our range was 18,000 yards," Hagen recalled.

Hagen was not used to being helpless. Usually he was the one dishing it out, but in this instance, he said to Evans, "Please, let's not go down before we fire our damn torpedoes." Evans gave him a grave nod and carried on with his work. "Do not bother me, do your best," Evans told Hagen.

Standing in the space behind the bridge, Hagen saw his captain work. "His heart was grinning as he went into battle. There was not a moment's hesitation or delay on his part." Evans pushed aside Ed DiGardi and Ellsworth Welch, his communications officers, and grabbed the wheel from the helmsman.

Evans kept his ship heading northwest as the carriers launched all aircraft; one jumped from the edge of a flight deck every forty-five seconds until the roughly twenty-five aircraft still aboard were aloft. Then the carriers would turn south in retreat as the *Johnston* continued northwest at high speed, laying smoke to cover their escape. As Evans pushed ahead at full speed toward the Japanese, he wrestled with the issue of his fuel supply. As with ammunition, there had not been a resupply in almost a week.

Most likely the *Johnston* would be struck by a shell in minutes and sink, so no shipyard bureaucrat would get mad at him for spoiling his engines, Evans determined. While at the helm, he ordered the chief engineer, Lieutenant Joe Worling, to pump the diesel into the fuel oil to expand the ship's endurance for what only *could* be a long battle. Mixing the two supplies would extend their engine life to four hours and would require cleaning only if they were alive long enough for it to matter.

The men on the bridge understood the need for this measure, though to Worling, whose "view of the ship was as an engineering plant," the mixing of fuel was not warranted under any circumstance. He climbed up to the bridge to consult the captain about the decision, but did not make it past the last step on the ladder. DiGardi and Hagen intercepted him. Hagen, who was still waiting to ascend into the director, yelled, "We're meeting the whole damn Jap fleet. Obey orders from the bridge!"

Mechanic's Mate Landreth later recalled that while he was mixing the fuels, "one of the chiefs in the engine room [was] saying that if we made it out of this we would be going back to the States for major repairs." However, the *Johnston* arguably being an engine wrapped in a thin skin gave her an edge against larger shells. Because the armor-piercing explosive shells would pass straight through without registering a hit, their explosive charges would not go off, resulting in less damage.

By 0705 Evans was still acting on his own. No order had been given to attack, though he was charging straight for the center of the twenty-three-ship armada. Only someone who was there could know the stress of the situation. Unable to shoot back—the range still needed to be reduced by six miles—Evans could hope only to remain undetected. The Japanese were not yet firing at the *Johnston*. They could not see her, for there were rain clouds blocking their field of view. The American pilots of Taffy 3 could see the destroyer, however, as they formed up to make their own attacks on the Japanese.

By 0708 the carriers had launched all aircraft and turned southeast, away from the Japanese. The *Johnston* had laid smoke over a twenty-five-hundred-yard front, though Japanese shells still fell accurately near the carriers. Startlingly the shells fired from fifteen miles away were visible to the eye as they roared overhead, and they fell almost vertically on the carriers. More shells might have struck home, but *Yamato* was able to fire only three-gun salvos. Her monstrous eighteen-inch guns had found the usable size limit of naval ordnance, for their powerful blast sheared deck riveting. As robust as she was, *Yamato* could have broken up if she had fired a full broadside.

To the American aviators organizing above, it appeared as if Evans were charging at the Japanese like a cavalryman of an earlier era. With every pound of steam pressure added inside *Johnston*'s two boilers, her speed grew, increasing the bow wake rising up around her hull. The Japanese vessels were to the northwest, arrayed from east to west with the easternmost units tailing up the map to the north, and the westernmost units hanging down to the south. At 0700 the southwestern flank of the Center Force had been fenced in by seven destroyers led by the light cruiser *Noshiro*. Then came the two battleships *Yamato* and *Nagato*, with *Yamato* leading. Farther northeast of these two was a third battleship, the *Haruna*. Below the *Haruna* came four destroyers, headed by the light cruiser *Yahagi*. East of the *Yahagi*, six heavy cruisers were in two columns: one column of four north of a column of two. North of the heavy cruisers was the battleship *Kongo*. The *Johnston* was twenty-four thousand yards east by southeast of the nearest Japanese unit, the heavy cruiser *Kumano*. The four battleships were in range, firing from between twenty-eight thousand and thirty-five thousand yards away—the *Kongo* was the closest—and as of 0706 their targets were still exclusively the Taffy 3 carriers.

Evans was still at the helm guiding the ship northwest. Behind him Hagen, still waiting to close distance, was standing in the space below the gun director. The closing speed between the

Johnston and the Japanese heavy cruisers, led by the *Kumano*, was almost sixty miles per hour. The *Johnston* had an effective firing range of fourteen thousand yards. On a straight course, the range would close in six minutes. The heavy cruisers, however, already had the *Johnston* within range and would change targets from the carriers to her by 0711, causing Evans to maneuver erratically.

The *Johnston*'s guns would be in range in nine minutes. After smoking a cigarette down to his fingers, Hagen tossed the butt onto the steel deck and reached for the ladder below the gun director. As he ascended into the director, he heard Evans's voice tearing through the others below him. Everyone had a part to play, and Evans was the stoic and zealous conductor of the action. All remembered the promise Evans had made on commissioning day, and they expected that he would fulfill it now.

Evans started the battle on the bridge next to the talker, who was at the rear of the bridge and had a direct link to Lieutenant Stirling and his men in the combat information center. There a battle map was being drawn independently of the ones forming in the minds of the crew. Understanding the spread of the enemy ships that they were attacking was crucial for their all-important task of preparing a torpedo run. Torpedo officers in the CIC labored to this end, communicating with Evans and his lookouts on the bridge as new information came on the radar.

DiGardi, positioned on the bridge as the communications officer during this battle, recalled that the battleships "were closing rapidly at 22–25 knots. Our carriers had a maximum speed of about 18." The first carrier to receive damage was the *White Plains*. A near miss sent a shock wave that dented her undercarriage and opened several minor leaks. Thousands of lives were at risk among the six retreating carriers, though the carriers in the most immediate danger were the two northernmost in formation: the *White Plains* and the *Fanshaw Bay*.

It was the carriers' good fortune that the *Johnston* had decisively begun to make funnel smoke, excess from the engine that poured from the ship's two stacks and clung to the sea. Orders were also given for chemical smoke. Pouring from generators on the fantail, this smoke was white, and it rose up toward the sky, further hindering the enemy's view of the targets. The plumes of smoke pouring from the *Johnston*'s two stacks marked her progress toward the enemy, and they appeared to stick to the sky, like gray paint strewn across a light blue canvas.

Evans's quick action in making a smoke screen increased the carriers' chances of survival, and his decision to turn north gave his own ship a greater chance of delivering a successful strike. During the golden minutes when the Japanese lustily fired at the carriers, the tiny *Johnston* went largely unnoticed and cut the distance rapidly. Lesser commanders would have waited to attack. "There was nothing like having a pro in charge," Lieutenant Welch remembered.

Another professional was "our gun boss, Bob Hagen . . . peering out of the gun director, ready for battle," Welch recalled. He had the best view. By 0710 Hagen was up and sticking his head out the metal hatch atop the gun director. Through binoculars he got his first close-up look at his enemy. The heavy cruisers were the closest Japanese ships. They were heading directly east toward the carriers, which by 0712 had reached the edge of a large rain squall that was being pushed west. The battleships were farther west; they were heading east toward the rain squall as well. Lower on the horizon, on either side of the battleships *Yamato* and *Nagato*, were the two destroyer columns. Hagen determined that they would attempt to make a torpedo attack later in the battle, but the main threat came from the heavy cruisers. It would be only a matter of time before they noticed the tiny destroyer, so Hagen kept his eyes on those closest Japanese ships. By 0712 their range was twenty thousand yards.

From the bridge Evans could see his forward two guns trained out toward the heavy cruiser column that was running east across their starboard bow. "Don't bother me, do your best," Evans had told Hagen before he rose to the gun director. This was effectively a standing order to open fire as soon as the range closed. Their range was just under eighteen thousand yards, though they were not accurate at more than fourteen thousand. Then Hagen would begin shooting. The destroyer's modern, synchronized guns were meant to be deadly accurate during this type of running gunfight.

By 0712 the carriers were concealed in the rain squall that had come from the east, but the *Johnston* was actively running away from it. Lookouts on the Japanese heavy cruisers then saw the *Johnston* charging toward them. The heavy cruisers were in two columns at 0712, but the *Chokai* and *Haguro* were slowing down to fall in line with the four heavy cruisers headed by the *Kumano* to their north. As the heavy cruisers formed a column—it would be safer to be in column once within the rain squall—they also trained their guns toward *Johnston*. As they did, a knot formed in Bob Hagen's stomach as he watched from the gun director.

Before lighting the cigarette between his lips, Hagen ordered the boy next to him to close the firing key. Then Hagen maneuvered the metal controls that pointed his fire director radar, angling the radar toward the Japanese heavy cruiser column. Once the first target was in his scope, there was nothing more for Hagen to do but wait, so he lit his cigarette, then pulled from it as the range dropped. "All this time I had been completely, sickeningly impotent. I had checked my gun stations, seen that everything was in order, but after that there was nothing I could do but wait," wrote Hagen. Below him Evans was waiting, too, but he was at the wheel and had more to do. Holding the ship on a course for the enemy, Evans began zigzagging as the heavy cruisers took aim at his destroyer.

Most of the crew were gritting their teeth, expecting to greet death at any moment. Men in the ammunition-handling rooms put faith in a higher power, saying silent prayers as their ship began maneuvering ever more sharply, but Bob Hagen counted on a different power. His god manifested itself in the tangible: trained men in the gun director, the swift handling of ammunition by sailors in the gunhouses, and the gyro-synchronized fire of his modern weapons.

After Hagen climbed into the director at 0710, Evans was on the bridge taking stock of the situation. There was rain to the west and Evans knew it would conceal him for a moment. The range was closing now to just over twelve miles, or twenty-one thousand yards. Quickly the distance dropped to nineteen thousand yards, and then the *Johnston* disappeared into a shadow of rain.

At 0714, when the *Johnston* emerged on the other side of this rain squall, the Japanese gunners on the heavy cruisers were looking for them. Splashes of water, tall columns colored red, erupted from near misses. Soon, in the sea nearby, exploding ordnance from the battleships *Yamato* and *Haruna* caused even larger geysers colored yellow and green to erupt. As in the Java Sea, the Japanese were using dye in their shells in order to tell where each ship was hitting. "The red, green, purple, and yellow colors might have been pretty under different circumstances, but at this moment I didn't like the color scheme," recalled Bob Hagen. Admiral Sprague apparently had similar thoughts because he later recorded of the battle that "the splashes had a kind of horrid beauty. No, I wouldn't say it was like a bad dream, for my mind had never experienced anything from which such a nightmare could have been spun."

On the bridge Evans began chasing splashes, spinning the wheel in the direction of the most recent, or largest, miss, a trick he had learned studying about the Battle of Jutland. Evans veered across the sea, hoping to avoid getting hit by the battleships' three-thousand-pound shells, which were soon joined by a hail of eight-inch shells from the cruisers. The closest threat was from the cruisers of the Seventh Division: the *Kumano, Suzuya, Chikuma,* and *Tone.* Behind them the *Chokai* and *Haguro* pushed on. Soon range was eighteen thousand yards, or ten miles, but Evans could not shoot back, despite the fact that shells from these six powerful cruisers—now in one column—landed nearby. They were going to cross the *Johnston's* T, passing east of them in their bid to reach the carriers. This course, Evans noticed, would make them an easy target for a wide-angle torpedo strike.

Torpedoes were Evans's greatest weapon, but he needed to get close. That was going to be tough. The Japanese battleship *Yamato* was zeroing in on the Americans, and the cruisers that they were attacking would not keep missing forever.

Fortune smiled on the Americans. At 0713 twenty torpedo

bombers dropped down through the cloud layer, opened their bomb bays, and attacked. Flying low and slow, they angled for an attack on the column of cruisers in an attempt to make the cruisers turn to evade, which would effectively slow them down. The sailors at the antiaircraft guns on the Japanese cruisers pounded away at the approaching torpedo bombers, furiously trying to knock them down. But they still came, braving the walls of flak that were put up.

After tense seconds the bombers reached their drop points and pulled up, though no payloads entered the sea. Japanese officers on the bridge were left dumbstruck because those pilots had obviously been bluffing. They'd had no torpedoes but risked their lives anyway.

Evans, meanwhile, continued chasing splashes, each column of water becoming his new heading. If his luck held, he would be able to connect the dots all the way to the enemy. "The Japanese fire was decidedly unimpressive. They should have sunk us immediately. Even so, their shells finally started straddling us," recalled Hagen. By 0714 the range was just over seventeen thousand yards.

Hagen was prepared to fight, having maneuvered his two metal handles and spun the director until he settled his scope on the nearest Japanese cruiser. Then, with his head stuck out the hatch at the top of the director, he would eye his target through his binoculars and observe the shooting of his guns, periodically glancing down at the men working within the confines of that metal box and checking that they were not experiencing any problems. He needed to know that they could clearly see the Japanese through their telescopes. With the easterly wind blowing at the back of Hagen's head—his hair kept in place by his khaki envelope cap—he could still hear Evans as he yelled course corrections to Ed DiGardi, who had been given the helm. This change gave Evans the opportunity to issue other commands more freely and to move to the bridge wings for different battlefield views. DiGardi would remain at the helm and maneuver as Evans directed for the remainder of the fight.

When Hagen wasn't standing with his head outside the gun director, he was sitting down in a metal bicycle seat in front of his periscope and metal control handles. To Hagen's right sat two officers, and behind him sat two others, each looking through a scope with an eight-degree field of view. When the other men's scopes lined up with the target that Hagen had in his sight, each man yelled, "On target!"

The *Johnston*'s fire control radar was first pointed at the lead heavy cruiser in the column of six. Hagen then yelled to another sailor next to him, "Close the firing key!" in case his order to do so earlier had not been recognized. With the firing key closed, the guns were allowed to fire at their own pace rather than wait for Hagen, who could fire the gun only in synchronized unison.

Before the clock hit 0715, Evans's war on the Japanese had begun. Underneath the five gun mounts, sailors began racing to put shells on the hydraulic hoists that fed the guns above them, and inside the gun mounts, men loaded these shells. It was a struggle to keep standing with the ship moving to evade shells and the turret rotating to match Bob Hagen's target; the range had now closed within sixteen thousand yards.

The air around the gun became shocked when the first cannon spat out a fifty-pound armor-piercing round, followed by a mushroom of cordite smoke and fire. There was a collective sigh of relief on the bridge that was masked by the aggressive barking of the five-inch guns, each of which could fire a shell every three to five seconds. The shooting made a terrible mess as used brass began to pile up on deck, and the unburned gunpowder casings that began to fall from the gun barrel quickly flew up in the faces of those on the bridge.

Once Hagen opened fire, the *Johnston* showed the full capacity of her main battery, landing on the *Kumano* no fewer than forty hits out of two hundred rounds—astonishing accuracy for that range—and starting fires on her superstructure.

The guns would not veer from their target as long as Hagen kept the fire control radar pointed at the *Kumano*. This radar would send signals to the fire control computer, which would interpret them and send electrical signals to the gun's hydraulically powered mounts. The guns automatically made corrections as the ship pitched and rolled, so each time Evans turned the ship to chase a new splash, the guns yawed to keep locked with the target that the fire control radar had marked.

After a few moments Hagen, opened the rate control key, allowing his guns to fire as soon as they were loaded, rather than waiting for a full salvo to be loaded. As the battle went on, the variance in loading time meant one to two seconds would be added between each salvo, so the guns fired at their own pace, increasing the ship's rate of fire by roughly fifteen rounds per minute. Belowdecks, men moved the twenty-eight-pound powder cases and the fifty-five-pound shells as fast as possible. In four minutes the *Johnston*'s five-inch guns would use their two hundred rounds of armor-piercing shells.

While the *Johnston* led her individual attack on the cruisers that were pressing in on the carriers from the northwest, two Japanese battleships and a column of destroyers about twenty thousand yards to the *Johnston*'s rear pushed their own attack from the west. At 0716 those battleships and destroyers, which had been consumed with an attack on the carriers, turned their guns toward the *Johnston* because smoke and rain had obstructed their view of the carriers. The heavy battleship guns creaked and groaned as they changed target from the carriers to the little escort bearing down on them just off their starboard bow. Meanwhile, the Japanese pursued by the *Johnston* were shocked to see a ship a fraction of their size closing in from their right side and attempting to stop them from pursuing the victory their emperor sought.

South of Evans, the captain of the destroyer *Hoel*, Commander Leon Kintberger, began his attack. He was the second destroyer captain to take initiative this morning, and at 0710 he had ordered his ship to make full speed for the Japanese. The *Johnston* had gone west, headed for the center of the Japanese force, but the *Hoel* headed directly north toward its eastern flank. The *Hoel* began the battle farther east than the *Johnston* and was in position to challenge the advance of the second pair of battleships.

Evans had commanded over the sound of his ship's automatic gunfire before, such as in Guam when his five guns had put out as many as forty rounds in a minute, but never before had he been receiving fire and steaming at full speed. Evans had to keep an ear out for any radioman with news from Admiral Sprague and the other ships, should an opportunity to coordinate arise.

As Hagen was opening fire on the *Kumano*, Evans gave Ed DiGardi orders to continue chasing splashes. Then he concerned himself with the efforts of Lieutenant Stirling, who, by phone from the combat information center, was communicating the best scenario for a torpedo attack.

The ideal angle for torpedoes to approach a target is sixty degrees relative to a target's bow. In order to have the best shot at hitting the enemy, Evans should have set his torpedoes to their maximum speed and released them from five thousand yards. The *Johnston*, however, only dared close to within ninety-five hundred yards of the leading cruiser and place its ten torpedoes at a forty-degree angle to the bow of the leading ship. Releasing his torpedoes at nearly ten thousand yards meant the enemy ship would be harder to hit, and releasing his torpedoes at a forty-degree angle to the target rather than at a sixty-degree angle would ensure that the enemy ship's full profile would not be exposed. It was the best he could hope for.

Evans then agreed with Lieutenant Stirling and his torpedo officer that one degree of separation was appropriate between each torpedo, and that torpedo mount one needed to be trained a hundred ten degrees relative to the ship's heading and mount two a hundred twenty-five degrees in order to be able to put the torpedoes in the water while the ship was farther into its turn and allow for a sharp retreat. Last, Evans needed to set torpedo depth. They were attacking larger ships, so a depth of six feet was ideal for flooding, as opposed to the torpedoes striking the heavy ships at three feet of depth and exploding against reinforced armor belts.

The cruiser division was heading due east at the time that Evans began making preparations for his torpedo attack. So *Johnston*, heading northwest, needed to cut to port and release torpedoes halfway through a hundred-eighty-degree turn. After agreeing to all the torpedo settings with Lieutenant Stirling in the CIC, Evans set the phone down and turned his full attention to their coming port turn.

The torpedo tubes were already trained out to starboard, prepared to launch once the distance closed. Above them Hagen kept himself busy. He intended to shift targets about every minute. By 0717 the first cruiser in column, the *Kumano*, was in flames from his pummeling. Hagen then yelled, "Changing target"—the signal that the men in the gun mounts should brace themselves while the fire control system electrically maneuvered their guns to match Hagen's fire control radar. Once on target, Hagen was careful to release the firing handle so that the guns did not follow any further direction from him as he searched for their next targets. There was a metallic click, like gears snapping into place, and the guns were on target.

The men in the gun turrets grew disoriented because they were rotated about their axis each time Hagen—maneuvering his metal controls—held in the firing handle and placed the fire control radar on a new target. The ship would land a few hits on a cruiser or destroyer, and then Hagen would yell, "Changing targets," and the guns would turn to his new bearing. This rhythm kept up during their run for the torpedo attack. Battleships and cruisers were bearing down from the north and northwest, and destroyers from the west.

———

At 0716 the Japanese on the bridge of the battleship *Yamato* lost their view of the carriers and began searching for other targets. The escort carriers were behind a veil of black engine smoke that clung to the ocean, white chemical smoke that rose above, and rain that was above the rest. Accordingly, lookouts on the battleships *Haruna* and *Nagato* shifted attention to the ship heading directly for their center.

At 0717 the *Haruna* spotted the *Johnston* and fired half a dozen shells, all missing, before the check-fire order came because the *Johnston* had disappeared again into a rain squall. Then at 0718 lookouts on the Japanese cruiser *Haguro*—east of the rain and in the *Johnston*'s field of vision—"sighted an enemy destroyer or cruiser [*Johnston*] bearing 43 degrees to starboard and closing." Its captain ordered main battery fire directed at the *Johnston*.

Evans was cutting across the ocean at nearly forty miles per hour, testing the crew's sea legs as he turned in to the gunfire. For the entire battle, once smoke cover began helping the carriers, no fewer than four Japanese ships were firing at the *Johnston* at any given time. The attackers were from the heavy cruiser column that approached Evans from the northwest, moving on a divergent and almost perpendicular course as they attempted to move east and close with the Taffy 3 carriers. "Looking through my telescope I could see the cruisers vengefully shooting at us," Bob Hagen remembered. "One 8-inch shell landed in the water right off our bow and splashed red dye in my face. I mopped the stuff out of my eyes."

The *Johnston* was drawing closer and Evans maneuvered more frequently. As Evans turned the ship, Hagen would shout down the ladder to Evans on the bridge, "What are you up to now?" Evans would stick his head into the space below the director and yell up to Hagen, "Take that ship!" Though Hagen did not always know to which ship Evans was referring, he understood that all were targets. Hagen would yell, "Changing target!" and his guns would follow his direction.

A half an hour into the battle, the aviators of Taffy 3 had launched numerous attacks. Mostly carrying hundred-pound bombs and five-inch rockets, the aircraft acted as mere nuisances to the armored Japanese warships. For pilots carrying only depth charges, the only way to score was to land a charge in the water near a ship's stern and have it jam the rudder.

Most fighters were armed with their full service load of ammunition. Even after bombs, rockets, and depth charges were used, these pilots bravely performed wave after wave of strafing gun runs against the Japanese. With fifty-caliber guns alone, some pilots made more than a dozen runs before retreating for nearby airfields or the carriers of Taffy 2, sixty miles south. Several aviators maneuvered their aircraft barely above the ocean surface with bomb doors open—flying low and slow, fooling Japanese warships into wasting their time with evasive turns, though in reality the American pilots carried no torpedoes.

There was no shortage of bravery this day. As the *Johnston* sped northwest toward the Japanese, Taffy 3 aviators circled and made dozens of hastily coordinated strafing runs. Nearly a hundred aircraft were winding through the sky, diving and running back into the clouds.

Blue Archer, an aviator flying off the *Kalinin Bay,* had a career day. It began questionably. He remembered getting soaked by Japanese shell splashes as he waited for his turn to take off, but after landing two five-hundred-pound bombs on a cruiser and emptying his machine guns, Blue Archer still had the hunger to open his canopy and fire six shots from his revolver at a Japanese battleship. Holding his revolver out his window, Archer savored the astonished look on the face of so many Japanese on that battleship's superstructure.

Evans stood on the bridge. Nearly everyone expected the ship to take a fatal hit at any moment. Every second the *Johnston* gifted the sailors on the carriers lowered the odds of her own crew's survival.

On the bridge Evans watched his target, the heavy cruiser *Kumano*. Though she was ablaze, he could see through his binoculars her eight-inch guns trained to starboard. Copper-orange flame erupted from her barrels, and three-hundred-pound shells roared through the air toward the *Johnston*. For years men who had been topside would remember the sight of the shells flying toward them, though they would also remember doing something about them.

The armor-piercing rounds that the *Johnston* had were capable of penetrating two inches into reinforced steel. The Japanese destroyers were not armored anywhere, and the Japanese light cruisers were exposed on their bridges. The Japanese heavy cruisers were protected at the waterline, so Hagen had to get repeat salvos in the same spot on the more lightly armored superstructures to penetrate them. With the range closing, this was possible, and Hagen was determined to get as many hits as he could with his remaining armor-piercing rounds. At their rate of fire, it would take less than five minutes to shoot all two hundred aboard. By 0718 the range was thirteen thousand yards and closing, and the cruisers in column astern or behind the *Kumano,* as well as the battered *Kumano* herself, fought back.

The intrepid men in the ammunition-handling rooms were making the fight. Four levels below Evans, these men were deprived of almost all information about the battle except the turning of the ship as Evans maneuvered to set up his torpedo strike. The sailors in the ammunition rooms labored to load the fifty-pound armor-piercing shells and later the thirty-three-pound antiaircraft shells onto the hydraulic hoists that fed the gun mounts. Once there the shells would be rammed into the chambers along with powder cases and sent through the muzzle.

While the *Johnston* was taking on the heavy cruisers, the two battleships *Yamato* and *Nagato* were farther to the west estimating their range. Near misses from the *Yamato* and *Nagato* violently shook the *Johnston.* The range to the *Yamato*—in the lead of the *Nagato*—was still twenty-three thousand yards, though for their massive eighteen- and sixteen-inch guns, respectively, the range seemed not to matter. The first salvo missed by a couple hundred yards but the towers of water were close enough to cause sailors on the *Johnston's* bridge to crane their necks and powerful enough to send waves rolling over the *Johnston's* side.

The torpedo mounts on the *Johnston* were trained out to starboard, and at 0720, she turned. In intervals, Evans ordered his torpedoes into the sea. "Fire mount one, fire mount two." Once the men at the torpedo mounts outside the ship phoned into the CIC that they had released all ten fish, Evans checked his watch.

In the belly of the ship, sailors were put at ease by what was unmistakably the motion of the *Johnston* coming about; their inner senses of balance were still functioning despite the concussions of their own guns above. The hundred-eighty-degree turn set the *Johnston* to the southwest, on course to cut across the turn of the retreating carriers.

By 0720 the carriers had turned south after initially heading east into the rain. The Japanese could not see the carriers for a few minutes, and this allowed them to turn south while the Japanese continued east, unaware that they could cut across the turn of the carriers.

Northeast of every Japanese unit was the battleship *Kongo*, separated from the other three battleships that were now forming together. *Kongo* was entering the northern arm of the rain squall, too, and would have limited visibility. West of the cruisers were the two destroyer columns, one to the north and one to the south and separated by five miles. Between them were the three other battleships: *Yamato* and *Nagato* in column, and *Haruna* moving independently, south of them, off their starboard side. The Japanese were blindly following the aircraft carriers into the rain, still unaware that the carriers had turned to the south. The other five Taffy 3 screening ships followed the carriers into the rain and on their southerly retreat, continuing to make smoke. The rain that now protected the carriers would soon protect the *Johnston* only if Evans could make it there without getting hit.

The *Hoel* closed range and became the second American ship to open fire on the Japanese. Commander Kintberger moved his destroyer at full speed, straight north in an attempt to head off the right flank of the Japanese. The *Hoel*, however, ran smack into the fast battleship *Kongo* defending the fleet's right flank. Quick shots from this battleship were received.

The *Hoel* received her first hits, two on the bridge, at 0725.

Then, a minute later at 0726, three more hits came, once each in the number two engine room, number two fire room, and number three ammunition-handling room. All power was lost for a moment until the diesel generator took over. Then Kintberger resumed at half speed, but the hits did not stop coming.

Dozens of shells hit in the water all around or went over the ship. Commander Kintberger, realizing that there were few scenarios in which they would be alive at the end of the battle, decided at 0727 to fire five of his torpedoes at the *Kongo* at a distance of nine thousand yards rather than wait. It was unclear if the *Hoel* would be alive long enough to fire her other five but Kintberger held out hope. The *Kongo* was accurate, and so great was the aim of the Japanese cruisers arrayed against her that by 0740 the *Hoel* had received a dozen direct hits from shells eight inches or larger in diameter.

At 0720 the *Johnston* had to wait seven minutes before her torpedoes were calculated to hit. If after those seven minutes there were no explosions, they would be misses. Though, like the *Hoel*, the odds that the *Johnston* would be afloat in seven minutes were not high. By 0720 all of the five-inch armor-piercing rounds were spent. Their initial gun run was over and they were in retreat. From now on they fired only proximity-fused antiaircraft rounds, which had the effect of peppering a ship's superstructure and killing men outside cover.

Evans exited to the port bridge wing and watched the battle develop. Ed DiGardi was still at the helm, but Evans ordered another sailor to take it and used DiGardi as a runner. He gave DiGardi course changes for the helmsman while he remained on the bridge wing.

Out there, Evans was joined by Welch and Lietuentant Bechdel, eager to observe the rewards of their attack. Rain clouds were being pushed in from the east. Off their port quarter—behind and to their left—the *Kongo* was concealed by spotty rain cover, and off their starboard quarter, the battleships *Yamato* and *Nagato* pressed their attack in column, followed by the *Haruna*. Directly north of the *Johnston* were the cruisers at which they had launched their torpedoes, but they were concealed within a rain squall, too. At this point Evans was making little effort to chase splashes. Though he still made evasive maneuvers, his main goal was to get back to the carriers as quickly as possible and make smoke.

Evans continued bellowing course changes, and Lieutenant DiGardi would run into the pilothouse and give them to the helmsman. Often before DiGardi was back to him, Evans would scream another order, sending DiGardi turning on his heels. For five minutes, as the *Johnston* pushed south, the large guns of the cruisers missed. Then, at 0725, Admiral Ugaki, commanding the *Yamato*, gave the order to engage the *Johnston*.

At the outset of battle, Admiral Sprague had ordered the American carriers east into the wind, then quickly changed heading toward the southeast and then directly south. It was supposed to be a self-sacrificial move. Aware that the Japanese could cut across their turn, Sprague reasoned that the move south would require Admiral Kurita to cover more distance in retreat, giving time for Taffy 2's pilots to strike. Sprague also wanted to keep himself "between the enemy fleet and our landing operations to the southwest," so he ultimately ordered Taffy 3 to the southwest. It was a gamble. Each of the turns the force made was done while within the cover of a rain squall that had blown in from the east.

Had even one of the Japanese leaders noticed the turn from the east, he could have cut across the wide turn of the carriers and sunk them before they had a chance to sneak west past the Japanese.

The Japanese, it seemed, were convinced that the carriers had kept an easterly course even after they had launched their aircraft. By 0730 Taffy 3 was heading toward the beaches of Leyte, where thousands of men and dozens of transports had been strewn across the sand to support the advance inland. But by 0730 the carriers had not yet snuck west past the Japanese. There was still time for the Japanese to discover the maneuver. While the destroyers and destroyer escorts in the screen continued to punch above their weight class, it was also important for them to keep the unknown movement of the carriers a secret.

Evans looked at his watch; nearly seven minutes had passed since he launched his torpedoes. Still unscathed, the ship churned water and carried her crew south by southeast.

Evans was alert. From the bridge he watched eagerly as the smoke and rain grew closer. They were salvation. The officers on the bridge could no longer see the Japanese cruiser they had targeted—they were concealed by rain, too—but they knew their torpedoes would soon land.

Men deep within *Johnston* heard two, possibly three underwater explosions when the torpedoes were scheduled to hit at 0727. Looking back, Evans saw the victim through the smoke; the cruiser *Kumano* was burning furiously. Her bow, struck just forward of where the armor plating began, had been blown clean off. *Kumano* immediately began losing speed as water rushed in. Soon the cruiser *Suzuya* overtook the *Kumano* and left the column to assist the other ship. The cruiser *Tone*, third in column, became the leader. With one blow two cruisers had been removed from the pursuit. Evans's victory was short-lived, however.

The *Johnston* was shaken violently by six hits landing within seconds of one another. To Evans it felt like he had been picked up out of the water and shaken by some invisible hand. Grave forces of physics could explain this violence. The hits came in two triple salvos, mere moments apart. First came three eighteen-inch shells from one of the main battery turrets of the super-battleship *Yamato*.

The first fell in a smashing arc and tore a three-by-six-foot hole in the main deck. The hole left the ceiling of two compartments exposed and water would pour through whenever the ship made a hard turn to starboard, which was often, as Evans continued to chase splashes. The shell traveled through the ship, ruptured steam and electrical lines, then detonated against the solid iron housing of the reduction gearbox in the second engine room—one of the only blocks of hardware on the *Johnston* heavy enough to detonate the hard-tipped armor-piercing round. This first hit reduced the ship's speed to seventeen knots and the first engine strained to maintain moderate speed.

The second eighteen-inch shell hit just farther forward of the first, landing one foot inboard on the main deck, penetrating, and hitting the main steam turbine. The steam that was released was eight hundred degrees; it killed almost everybody in the second engine room. The door separating the handling room for the two aft five-inch guns from the second engine room was blown open, and it killed men in this position, though the handling room was reactivated once the number two engine was shut down temporarily. The massive concussion of the shell exploding opened seams in the hull, and flooding began.

The third and final eighteen-inch shell penetrated and entered the number two engine room. The *Johnston* was dead in the water until repairs to the pipes in the first engine room could be fixed to prevent steam from harming the men inside, but the equipment in the first engine room was operational. The *Johnston* carried on with split plant operation, deriving all of her power from the first engine.

What had moments before been a full sprint in retreat turned into a slow roll forward. As the destroyer slowed, water splashed up over the stern as the ship's wake quickly caught up to her. Then, mercifully, the *Johnston* reached the rain squall. While in the rain, the crew briefly attempted to route power to the second engine, though this caused electrical fires, and after the crew realized that the power lines had been cut, no further attempt was made to start the second engine.

The combined weight of these three eighteen-inch shells was just under five tons, but still the *Johnston*'s back was not broken. But then she was hit by a full salvo of six-inch shells. The moment that passed between these two salvos was surreal. Some recollected them as simultaneous blows; others recalled the interval between hits as many long seconds.

Standing and barely composed, Evans had been shaken violently by the first salvo; he traded glances with the other men on the bridge, and thought that they had survived their first hit unscathed. Then two six-inch shells hit the port side of the bridge, injuring Evans and killing others. A third hit the number two stack just below the secondary gun director station. The ship rolled violently, causing the radar antenna, capable of withstanding two thousand pounds of shock, to snap and fall over the ship. The wound looked dramatic but added only superficially to the state of the ship. Hagen and the men in the fire director were unharmed, but the bridge crew had been ravaged.

Lieutenant (jg) Ed DiGardi recalled that "during the run in and upon retirement Els [Welch] and I were on the port wing of the bridge with Bechdel, the Captain and our Squadron Recognition Officer. The Captain gave me orders for a course change so I went into the pilot house, followed by Els. About 10 seconds later we took our first hits. I returned to the bridge to carnage." In those ten seconds, all six of these shells landed.

Lieutenant Welch recalled that when he entered the pilothouse behind DiGardi, a shell exploded behind him. "We ended in a pile of humanity." Edward Block, the ship's troublemaker, had left his useless AA gun to be useful. Block was blown across the pilothouse and came to rest against the starboard wall. He went unconscious for a moment.

Blown also from the wing of the bridge, "Lt. Jack Bechdel was propped against the wheelhouse, complaining about injuries to his lower arms not aware that his legs had been blown off." To relieve his pain Welch gave Bechdel morphine before he was hauled one deck below to the officers' wardroom, which had become a makeshift operating room.

In addition to Bechdel's mortal wound, Ensign Gordon Fox and Lieutenant (jg) Joe Pliska, who had been standing next to Captain Evans, had been killed outright. According to Hagen, the bridge looked like a kid's BB gun target. The bridge had been hit by two six-inch shells; if they had been eighteen-inch shells like the one that had destroyed their number one engine, Evans and everyone on the bridge would have died that instant. It was 0729 when a sense of place returned to the bridge.

All the survivors on the bridge were concussed. "The skipper was standing bareheaded and bare-chested. His helmet and all but the shoulders of his shirt had been blown away; the hair on his chest was singed and blood was gushing from his left hand where two fingers had been shot away. Shell fragments ripped his neck and face. The doctor rushed to his aid, but the skipper waved him back saying 'Don't bother me now. Help some of those guys who are hurt.'" Evans wrapped a bandage around the stumps of his fingers and carried on.

Clarence Trader was assigned to a 40mm antiaircraft gun just below the bridge on the starboard side. Trader was awakened from a state of shock when he heard, "Block is alive." Trader looked behind him and saw blood flowing like water from the bridge, and then he heard Evans begin to shout to begin collecting bodies.

Once composed, Evans ordered DiGardi to get the engine room on the phone. He needed a report. "We were dead in the water and had lost steering and engine power," DiGardi recalls. Steering did not return because the electrical lines had been cut and could not be reestablished because of spontaneous electrical fires. When the crew attempted to route energy to the rudder, fires spread. Steering had to be performed manually, Evans learned, so he began shouting from the bridge, requesting sailors from useless gun mounts to report to the manual steering room in the fantail. Clarence Trader heard this order and ran to the fantail, where Clyde Burnett was gathering men to work in shifts muscling the rudder during the rest of the battle.

In the rudder control room, men from useless stations—such as the depth charge racks—were shifting the ship's rudder, turning it like pirates of an earlier time. The work was exhausting. The device that needed moving was a wheel attached to a vertical bar that ran down through the deck and connected to the rudder. Entering the steering gear room through a hatch on the fantail, men from useless stations would take shifts executing turns being ordered by Evans on the bridge. Soon one engine returned and carried the *Johnston* into the rain. The battleships and destroyers to the west and the cruisers to the north all disappeared as visibility dropped.

Hagen recalls the saving grace of the rain squall. "It was sheer providence. We ducked into it. I remember that it got my cigarettes wet; it was the first time in my life I didn't mind having a package of cigarettes ruined." A crew member stationed belowdecks recalled that "while in the rain squall, some of us went topside for a few minutes for a look. It was bad." Unknown bodies lay all about the deck and bits of shrapnel covering the deck gave the appearance of a small village recently covered with volcanic debris.

The *Johnston* had not exposed herself in vain. The torpedo attack had knocked the bow off the cruiser *Kumano*, which, without her bow, had her speed reduced to twelve knots. Ultimately this cruiser and the one behind her, the *Suzuya*, pulled back. The work of the torpedomen, Evans, and his executive officer in the moments before their attack would earn them a hero's welcome back home.

Bob Hollenbaugh, the gun captain to the fourth main gun, gun 54, was a hero of the Battle of Leyte Gulf, too. After the Japanese shells pounded the *Johnston*, Hollenbaugh recalled that "all sound in my earphones went dead. After unsuccessful attempts at contacting the Main Battery Director, I popped my head out the gun captain's hatch on top of the mount and asked the crews of the 40mm gun director (immediately forward my hatch) to see if they could get permission for us to fire Gun 54 in local control."

Soon enough Hollenbaugh's message reached Hagen and "permission was granted and Gun 54 declared its own war on the Japs," Hollengaugh recalled. All Hollenbaugh had to do was stick his head out of the top hatch and listen to shouts from the secondary director for bearing and elevation numbers, which he then shouted into the gun mount, all the while praying that his head would not be knocked off by shrapnel the next time he stuck it out of the hatch to hear another pair of coordinates. Hollenbaugh could not see the Japanese, though the shooting coordinates fed from the secondary director would give him an idea of their position. Hollenbaugh could also mimic the firing of gun 55, which was still being fed accurate coordinates from the gun director, though it was no longer making automatic range adjustments because its hydraulic system had been knocked out.

Hagen knew the cover would not last. "I had to take all this in quickly, for I had work to do. 'All stations, control testing!' I yelled, waiting anxiously to learn the damage. They came back, 'Gun One Aye! . . . Gun Two Aye! . . . Gun Three Aye! . . . Gun Five Aye!' All answered but No. 4. In a few seconds I heard from it. The Gun Captain, a smart lad named Bob Hollenbaugh, sent a messenger to another station to notify me his communications were out." Guns 1 and 2 still had power and moved with the assistance of hydraulics; guns 3, 4, and 5 were without power and had to be manually maneuvered, cranked by hand from within. Gun 4 was in the worst condition. Being cut off from the director and the plot, which fed target coordinates to the gun, its crew would aim by eye. Immediately after his guns reported back to him, Hagen, with help from Lieutenant Stirling and a radarman in the CIC, centered the fire control radar on the Japanese cruisers to the north. It was now 0732.

While the ship was hiding in the rain, its guns fired more than one hundred rounds at the nearest Japanese cruiser. They had reached the end of their armor-piercing supply, and they fired antiaircraft rounds instead.

On the bridge Evans labored to tend to the wounded and remove the bodies. While he went about addressing this work, he assessed the risk of remaining in command from there. Should he give orders from the wrecked bridge? There was no visibility. The rain around them blocked the view of the surrounding battle that threatened to surround and swallow the now crippled *Johnston*. By 0735 the ship was at half speed and the *Yamato*, *Nagato*, and *Haruna* were all approaching from the west at full speed. They could not see the *Johnston*, but now firmly between the Japanese battleships, she was where the Japanese believed the American carriers to be while they moved through the rain. However, the *Haruna* was surprisingly accurate.

Though there was no visibility now, remaining on the bridge would give Evans the best position to see the battle when they exited from the rain. The problem with remaining on the bridge was that steering control had been lost. Runners accomplished short-term needs while men labored to set up a direct phone line to the after steering room. In the rain the sound of thundering gunfire was heard in the distance as Japanese ships searched for the carriers of Taffy 3.

The bridge was soon cleared of bodies. Evans was giving erratic steering commands. They were still in the rain and heading west by southwest, though Evans would soon change course to the south as he realized because of radar readings that the carriers had turned to the southwest. The radar also showed that at between eleven and thirteen thousand yards, a force of Japanese ships was closing. These were the battleships. They were moving north of the *Johnston*, on course to cross over to the east of her, but they still could not see her. The *Yamato* led the *Nagato* and *Haruna* in column. The *Haruna* had landed five salvos near the *Johnston* at 0734, though by 0736 she had lost sight of the U.S. ship. The *Yamato* and *Nagato* were unaware of her location in the rain and held their fire.

The deck was still filled with debris, though at first glance the only material damage was to the main mast antenna, which had fallen. As sailors placed the wires that would carry Evans's steering orders to the after steering room, runners jumped past them, carrying the next messages. Runners would continue to brave the gauntlet of the debris-covered and rain-slickened deck until Evans's communications with the fantail were secured by the hastily rigged phone line.

As the time crept on, now 0745, the *Johnston* was still in the rain. To her east the *Hoel* was also maneuvering at half speed after taking dozens of direct hits. The destroyer escort *Raymond*, east of Taffy 3 at the start of shooting, opened fire on the Japanese at 0740 once the range closed to 14,080 yards. Their captain, who had until now remained with Taffy 3 in hopes of coordinating a strike with the other destroyer escorts, headed west to cover the carriers' move to the southwest. By now the destroyer escort *Dennis* was also headed west, laying smoke for the carriers, and she would begin shooting as soon as range closed to fifteen thousand yards, which would not happen until 0750.

In the *Johnston's* CIC, Lieutenant Stirling watched the radar receiver. Japanese battleships were now directly north of them, expecting to reach the other end of the rain squall and find the carriers. The cruiser column the *Johnston* had engaged with had reached the other side of the rain ahead of the battleships. It sent an urgent message for Admiral Kurita aboard *Yamato*. The carriers were not there, but instead were eleven miles to the south, moving toward Leyte. The *Johnston* was not there either when the cruisers reached the eastern end of the rain squall. She was heading south, still concealed within the center mass of the rain that was pushing west by southwest.

The *Haruna* spotted the *Johnston* occasionally through the rain. By 0750 the Japanese force had turned southeast. Time was running out for the carriers. Time was also against the *Johnston*. Every starboard turn that Evans took put more water into the two exposed compartments, making each turn more strenuous for the men who worked to turn the rudder by hand.

CHAPTER 12

"Now I've Seen Everything"

OCTOBER 25, 1944, 0743–1015

At 0743—twenty-three minutes after Evans had fired all ten of his fish—Admiral Sprague's order for the screen to make a torpedo attack came. The *Hoel*, after firing her first spread of torpedoes, turned and headed back south, but then was crushed beneath a fusillade of heavy shells, limiting her to half speed. She fell behind, becoming stuck among Kurita's fleet, which had pushed its advance southeast. The four remaining heavy cruisers were on *Hoel*'s left along with the battleship *Kongo*, and the battleships *Yamato*, *Haruna*, and *Nagato* were to *Hoel*'s right. The *Johnston* was to the southwest, inside the rain squall, which was still drifting to the west.

At 0748, while the destroyer *Heermann*, *Johnston*'s fellow-*Fletcher*, and the four destroyer escorts were forming to attack, the *Hoel* began her second attack, intending to push the battleships off course. The *Yamato* and *Nagato* were traveling southeast in column, overtaking the *Hoel* from the northwest. Kintberger's turn was sharp. He swung to starboard, lined up his spread with the column's path, and fired his five remaining fish at the *Yamato*. Japanese lookouts spotted the *Hoel*'s torpedoes quickly, and the *Yamato*'s commander made a stunning mistake. Reactively, Ugaki turned to port to avoid the torpedoes. The *Nagato* followed his lead, and the two battleships plowed toward the northeast, running between the *Hoel*'s torpedoes.

Having made their turn, the *Yamato* and *Nagato* could not come back to the south without risk of being struck. Had Ugaki turned to starboard, as one would have expected of an aggressive commander with a death wish, the battleships would have combed the torpedoes equally well and still closed on the American carriers. As it was, for several critical minutes, they raced northeast, away from the action. Those moments "felt like a month to me," Ugaki recalled. He was never quite able to close range again, a blessing that Admiral Sprague was quick to realize: "The escorts turned the battleship fleet away momentarily and created a diversion of immense value."

It was now, at 0750, that Evans noticed the other five escorts begin their torpedo attack. Evans was himself out of torpedoes, but his fire control radar still worked, so he stood in bravely to steal the attention of the Japanese.

Still in the director, Hagen heard Evans shout, "[W]e will fall in behind them and provide fire support." They were out of armor-piercing rounds. "Fire whatever you have," Hagen ordered his gun captains. Their antiaircraft shells had built-in radar transmitters that triggered detonation within ten yards of a target. These highly advanced proximity-fused projectiles were very useful in showering airplanes with hot shrapnel, but apart from inflicting superficial damage to superstructure, they were unable to wound an armored warship. These shells would, however, act like the grape-shot of a previous era, and exposed flesh would be shredded by what remained in the *Johnston*'s magazine.

"The *Johnston* certainly could have retired with honor," Hagen remembered of their own torpedo run. However, Evans once again ordered a hard-left rudder, bringing them back on course for the Japanese. The extended port deflection of the rudder gave a break to those men manually steering the ship. As the *Johnston* turned back toward the Japanese, the men in the aft steering room had nothing to do for a few moments.

Despite Evans's willingness to sacrifice his ship, he knew very well that the *Johnston* could not land any serious punches. "We felt like little David without a slingshot," Bob Hagen wrote later. What they could do was draw fire away from the others, and Evans heard the thundering of his two forward guns, still connected to the gun director and both with functioning hydraulic controls.

At this moment Evans had a change of heart. Providing fire support for the others came at the cost of his primary assignment: protect the carriers. Was it better to continue charging in again and perhaps give the other escorts a chance to further harass the oncoming enemy, or to fall back and lay more smoke to obscure the vulnerable flattops? Two battleships had been deflected to the north, but two more, *Kongo* and *Haruna*, were still closing in. After a moment's calculation, Evans barked to pass the order down to the men in the steering compartment to continue their port turn. *Johnston* wheeled three hundred sixty degrees and came back south toward the carriers, laying smoke as she went, the generators on the fantail churning out white smoke while the stacks spat out black smoke.

Many men, mostly from the damaged engine room, had left their posts after a hopeless fight with the electrical fires, and gone on the deck. One of these men got word to Evans that other men were trapped below. This got Evans running to the starboard bridge wing, where he shouted for any men with knowledge of the engine room to search for men trapped there. It was dark down there and Evans knew the engine spaces were a labyrinth of hot, bent metal.

Even after the *Yamato* and *Nagato* turned away, the *Haruna* still pressed southeast and was positioned off the *Hoel*'s starboard quarter, behind and to the right of the *Hoel*, which was retreating south. At 0750, with her speed reduced to half, the *Hoel* barely edged across the front of the *Haruna*'s path. The *Hoel* had escaped barely what could have been a gauntlet of fire from the Japanese. Once clear of that killing zone, the *Hoel* began to retreat to the southwest on a straight course to meet up with the carriers of Taffy 3. The *Hoel* hugged the eastern edge of another rain squall and hid from the view of the battleships. However, the four cruisers could still see the *Hoel*, and they did not let up firing on her.

Between the *Hoel* and the heavy cruisers came the *Raymond* and *Heermann* cutting west across the path of the heavy cruisers and battleship *Haruna*. They had come charging north ahead of the *John C. Butler*, *Dennis*, and *Samuel B. Roberts* after Sprague gave the order. Between the *Heermann* and the four destroyer escorts, Taffy 3 had twenty-two more torpedoes to use.

When the *Heermann* made her attack at 0754, the *Sammy B.* was three thousand yards to her southeast. The *Raymond* would make her attack two minutes later from four thousand yards west of the *Heermann*.

Aboard the *Samuel B. Roberts*, Commander Copeland was maneuvering north, heading along the rain squall's southern boundary. He would pass unseen around the rain's eastern edge. The *Samuel B. Roberts* held her fire because her captain knew not to give away his position, a strategy similar to Andrew Jackson's tactics at the Battle of New Orleans. The *Samuel B. Roberts* snuck in close, and at 0756, Copeland exposed his ship momentarily and fired her three torpedoes; they were aimed at the cruiser *Haguro*, which was fifty-three hundred yards away and heading southeast in the lead of the entire Japanese formation. Because the *Sammy B.*'s speed-setting wrench had been blown away by a shot from the Japanese, its torpedoes could not be fired at their maximum speed. As a result, they missed the *Haguro*. While the *Samuel B. Roberts* was retreating from the torpedo attack, its gunners scored direct hits on the cruiser *Haguro*'s number two turret, killing thirty men and causing terrible fires.

At 0756 the destroyer escort *Raymond* launched her three torpedoes four miles from the column of heavy cruisers, which avoided them. Two minutes later at 0758, the *Heermann*—after running due west at full speed for two minutes—fired her three remaining torpedoes at the battleship *Nagato*, and turned away as the *Nagato* took evasive maneuvers.

Seven thousand yards to the southwest of the *Sammy B.*, the destroyer escort *Dennis* launched its three torpedoes at 0800. The target was the battleship *Haruna*, which was moving southeast toward the suspected location of the carriers. Those torpedoes missed. Farther southwest the *John C. Butler* was engaging six Japanese destroyers headed by the light cruiser *Noshiro*; *Butler* fired its two five-inch guns from less than twelve thousand yards.

At 0805 the *Johnston* was pushing south through the rain squall when the crew had another paralyzing experience. Though Evans was looking for the Japanese, he could see little else but smoke. Suddenly, two hundred yards away, he spotted the *Heermann* returning to the carriers from her own torpedo attack. Evans yelled, "All engines back full!" The *Johnston* had only one engine and could merely slow down.

In the director Hagen could see the unavoidable collision. "I felt a curious, hopeless, detached sort of wrung-out unconcern as I looked over our bow and couldn't see water—only the *Heermann*," Hagen recalled. *"I Hope we don't batter her up too much."* The *Heermann*'s two engines were enough to back her up, though, and a potentially disastrous collision was avoided by less than fifteen feet.

"Spontaneous cheers rose up from all sailors on the decks of both destroyers." Then out of the smoke came the *Samuel B. Roberts*, returning from her own torpedo attack. The view had been cleared of smoke, so collisions with both the *Johnston* and *Heermann* were avoided by several hundred yards.

After the *Johnston* backed away from the *Heermann* and the *Samuel B. Roberts* passed, Evans again increased his steam and headed south. Evans did not have a picture of his surroundings, only below in the combat information center did Elton Stirling have an idea of where other ships were, though he wasn't sure about the identities of all of them. There were eleven ships closing from the north; those were certainly the enemy. Evans wanted to continue concealing the carriers' southwest movement. To the east there were several radar signatures, and it was uncertain which ships they were, so Evans ordered Hagen to cease fire unless he could see his target.

Evans could see five hundred yards in the rain. He kept his eyes peeled to port, and looked back behind him often for the ships coming from the north that Lieutenant Stirling saw on the radar. There was also a contact directly to the east that got Evans's attention. Because the radar could not deduce the size and nationality of the radar contact, Hagen held his fire.

The sea was dark. Suddenly, like a lost city, a great towering structure appeared. Hagen was looking at the pagoda mast of a battleship—the pagoda mast was enough to identify the warship as Japanese. From two miles away, he couldn't see the entire ship. It was the *Haruna*, which had hugged the eastern face of the rain squall in a bid to reach the carriers sooner than the cruisers that had traveled farther east to get around the rain.

Hagen remembered saying to himself, "I sure as hell can see that," and focusing the fire control radar. From two miles away, the *Haruna* could not depress her guns enough to hit the *Johnston*. Instead, shells sailed overhead while the *Johnston* put more than thirty antiaircraft shells into the *Haruna*'s superstructure in under forty seconds. It was like bouncing wads of paper off a steel helmet, so Evans turned the *Johnston* back into the rain, leaving the *Haruna* to edge out of the rain and continue searching for the carriers where they would not be. It was 0810 as Evans approached the southern edge of the rain squall.

Outside the rain, the battle had developed. Cruisers would be the main threat to the *Johnston* as she exited the rain squall. They had made it to the eastern edge of the rain, seen no carriers, and turned south in search. Destroyers, too, from the northwest would be dangerous, though they were still north of the rain and would be kept at the edge of their effective firing range for another half hour. Farther north of the destroyers, the battleships *Yamato* and *Nagato*, which had been able to turn around only at 0804 after the *Hoel*'s torpedoes ran out of fuel, were heading back south.

By 0810 the *Johnston* was out of the rain, and the four heavy cruisers left in column, which were only twelve thousand yards off her port beam, had good shots. Once out of the rain, the battleship *Haruna* had a fresh look at the slowed *Johnston*, too, and the *Yamato*, now heading southeast, had fleeting glimpses at the *Johnston* through the rain.

The hull of Evans's destroyer began taking a beating from the shock of near misses, and this complicated the efforts of his rescue parties belowdecks. Men in asbestos suits were grabbing sailors from the second engine room, but they became concussed from underwater explosions. The Japanese shells were designed with .4-second fuse delays, providing them with more penetrating power before explosion. This also meant that if they missed their mark, they could still explode in the water and wreak havoc on a ship's underside.

At last, the American escort carriers began to be overtaken, and the Japanese quickly found their marks. At 0750 the carrier *Kalinin Bay* took her first hit. From the Japanese point of view, the carrier *Kalinin Bay* seemed to disappear behind the towers of water sent up by missed shots. At 0750 the carrier *Fanshaw Bay* received two hits from a heavy cruiser; both eight-inch shells hit the deck and tore through the maze of compartments below before exiting out the side.

The American escorts had put up a valiant fight. So had the American aviators. The timing could not have been better when, at 0800, aircraft from the other Taffy units began to show up for the fight. "By golly, I think we may have a chance," recalled Taffy 3's commander about this time. The Japanese cruiser numbers were short the *Kumano* and *Suzuya*, with two more burning from bomb hits from aircraft of Taffy 2.

By 0818 the *Johnston*, almost unbelievably, had reengaged the heavy cruisers. From the bridge Evans could see the Japanese; they were only seven miles away. The *Chokai* took the rear; her damage from the *Samuel B. Roberts* caused her to slow down and fall out.

From the north a column of destroyers fired on the *Johnston*, and the battleship *Kongo*, which had remained far to the north, gained sight of the *Johnston* after the rain cleared. The *Johnston*, it seemed, was being gained on. "We were taking hits and giving out hits at this time. Everybody was making smoke and a melee developed," recalled DiGardi. Every time the guns fired, the empty shells would get spat out onto the deck. It got to the point where most guns could not rotate without knocking over a pile of brass.

Evans was becoming surrounded. Destroyers were to their right and battleships and cruisers to their left. The armored superstructure of the *Tone* had been receiving the *Johnston*'s attention until the *Chikuma* began landing accurate hits on the *Johnston*. "We shifted fire and managed to pump at least ten shells into her," Hagen recalled.

Gun 52 took a direct hit around 0820 and fires raged on the

ship. Evans had the horror of seeing the hit, and shrapnel from it brushed the bridge. "One or two of the gun crew was literally blown out of the hatch on the starboard side of the mount," recalled Hagen. Clouds of smoke blew back and combined with the unburned powder that was flying up onto the bridge from the forward two guns; those on the bridge found their vision badly obscured. Hagen remembered, "[T]here was so much smoke that the skipper ordered me not to fire at anything unless I could see the ship." Black smoke poured from gun 52, burning Evans's eyes and Hagen's above him.

———

At 0817 the *Gambier Bay* received its second hit, a glancing blow off the flight deck. At 0820 the *Gambier Bay* received a third shell hit, which created serious flooding in the engine room. At 0824 she received hits four and five, both below the waterline, increasing her flooding. Her speed was reduced to eleven knots, and she began to fall behind. At 0828 the *Gambier Bay* received another hit, and another eighteen-inch shell at 0830 slammed directly through the flight deck.

After gun 52 was hit, there was not much Evans could see. He looked around squinting, searching for friend or foe. Evans could make out the lines of the *Saint Lo* and *Gambier Bay*, the two northernmost carriers, which were just seven miles south of him, shielded by a weak rain squall. Aside from the rain, the carriers were shielded by the towering geysers rising around them as the Japanese landed their delayed-fused armor-piercing shells in the water. Certainly, the carriers were dealing with significant undersea trauma from the near misses. Evans was on course to join them though he could not know if he would; the carriers were moving southwest at their full speed of twenty knots and the *Johnston* was moving south at seventeen knots with only one good engine.

The Japanese had not turned south until they gained the eastern edge of the rain squall that had run through the battle scene during its first hour. The Japanese waited to turn south and effectively followed Taffy 3 while they headed east, then south, then southwest. Taffy 3 had entered the rain moving east but exited moving southwest. The Japanese did not learn this until after the rain had passed.

Now there were no Japanese units to the west of the *Johnston*; directly north of the *Johnston*, two Japanese destroyer columns were heading south. The destroyers landed hits on the *Johnston*, though there was no longer an imminent threat that they could cut across the southwest turn of the carriers. Off the *Johnston*'s port side at seven miles were the four remaining heavy cruisers, and three miles beyond the cruisers were the two battleships, *Haruna* and *Kongo*. The *Yamato* and *Nagato* were twelve miles to the northeast, still closing distance after the *Hoel*'s torpedo attack had forced them to run in column away from the fight for about nine minutes. The carriers were traveling southwest in a circular formation. The escorts were running back to them, laying smoke.

On the bridge Evans peered through shattered windows. Black smoke was pouring from the ruined mess of gun 52 in front of him, though he still found it workable to command from the bridge. Now clear of the rain, Evans looked around and took in the battle's progress since he had entered the rain at 0735. It was now 0815.

For twenty minutes Evans continued south, firing at Japanese destroyers to the rear and heavy cruisers to the left with little effect. The battleship *Kongo* also took sporadic aim at the *Johnston* from about 0822 to 0826. However, the heavy cruisers were the main threat to the carriers and the *Johnston*.

The cruisers were vying to move south of the American carriers and cut west to trap them between the eleven destroyers that were moving down directly north of the carriers and threatening to break west of them. Five of the six escort carriers moved southwest at twenty knots, pushing to avoid being overtaken by cruisers to their left and destroyers to their right. The Japanese were closing fast, though all the carriers had hopes of keeping distance between them and the Japanese, all except the *Gambier Bay*.

Evans moved between the bridge and the starboard wing, keeping an eye on the destroyers approaching behind them from the north. His rear gunners engaged the destroyers, while his forward guns engaged the cruisers. The fight with the cruisers was not going well. The distance was at the edge of their effective range and would be until the cruisers made their move west, which they were sure to do. Five miles south of Evans was the *Gambier Bay*. She was on fire and had taken on a ten-degree list. By 0831 the Japanese cruiser *Tone* edged her bow south of the *Gambier Bay* and drifted west in preparation to turn the column in pursuit. Soon the entire heavy cruiser column would have the southern edge of the *Gambier Bay* and be in position to cut west and overtake her.

Evans considered his obligation to his crew, then thought of the thousands aboard the carriers. Without another thought, Evans shouted up to the director, "Commence firing on that cruiser [the *Tone*]. Draw her fire on us and away from the *Gambier Bay*." With a sinking feeling in his stomach, Bob Hagen oriented the director to find this cruiser in his scope.

Hagen yelled down, "Changing targets," and Evans watched as his forward two guns swung out. Soon Hagen observed through his scope several shells wrack the *Tone*'s bridge, though the *Johnston* was no more than a pest. However, by 0830, no fewer than eighteen of the twenty-three Japanese ships were firing on the *Johnston*. Still, it seemed that no amount of shooting could take the *Tone*'s attention.

Evans observed with a sense of melancholy, declaring out loud, "What fools." The heavy cruiser captains had the upper hand; they could have sunk the *Johnston* and the *Gambier Bay* at the same time. Evans seemed to want the Japanese cruiser captains to take him on. Evans ordered the ship to remain heading south, instead of turning southwest to join the other five retreating carriers. By 0834 the four heavy cruisers were cutting west, closing with the stricken *Gambier Bay*. The *Johnston* fired back and laid smoke.

The wind pushed the smoke west. But not all Japanese units were east of the smoke. Up in the gun director, Hagen noticed a destroyer column exit the rain to the *Johnston*'s northwest. At 0834 their range was ten thousand yards; by 0835 the range was cut to ninety-five hundred yards, almost torpedo range. The Japanese destroyers—seven of them in column behind the light cruiser *Yahagi*—would close on the carriers if unchallenged.

The seven destroyers were firing and hitting the *Johnston* all over. Belowdecks, fires caught and burned, forcing many men to come topside and look for places to hide, but all of the men on deck were exposed. There was nowhere to hide. The areas under-neath and behind the gun mounts were used to shelter the wounded, so the healthy men could only lie down on deck and hope not to be cut up by shrapnel.

Crew members from belowdecks, the antiaircraft mounts, and the now useless torpedo racks gathered in the ship's midsection. There was a lot of space below the torpedo mounts, and men gath-ered there, but suddenly a shell exploded in this space, igniting one of the 40mm ammo lockers. Exploding shells sent liquid fire flying, killing everyone huddled between gun 53 and the second torpedo mount.

With the director trained north, Hagen had a view of the aft section of the *Johnston*. He saw the hit from the destroyer leader send metal and limbs flying. Unable to calm his nerves with a cigarette—they had been ruined in the rain—Hagen set himself to the task of revenge. At 0840 the range closed to seventy-five hundred yards and Hagen changed target from the cruisers to port to the destroyers approaching the *Johnston*'s right.

First the *Johnston* landed twelve devastating hits on the de-stroyer leader, which quit cold, turned ninety degrees to port, and retired from the fight. Then the *Johnston* took on the second de-stroyer and scored five hits before it turned to follow the first.

Belowdecks, sailor Bob Sochor sweated inside an asbestos suit, hoping to find survivors in the after fire room. It was hot and steamy, and there was no light save for a battle lantern Sochor car-ried with him, but he found a man. Not certain if the man was alive or dead, Sochor tied a rope around him, and men on the deck above hauled him topside.

Then Sochor went back down into the heat and black smoke,

though the smoke had grown thicker and his light could not penetrate more than a few feet. He gave up the search. Back on deck
Sochor began to head for the fantail to take a turn shifting the
rudder, but to his surprise, the hatch he had just exited from the
after engine room began to turn. When it opened a sailor stum-
bled out, sweating after withstanding the heat of boiling steam for
more than ten minutes. This sailor, it turned out, had climbed
down underneath some grating and hugged the hull of the ship,
allowing the metal of the *Johnston's* hull, cooled by the ocean tem-
perature, to keep him safe. This man needed medical attention.
Sochor brought him to the makeshift hospital in the officers'
wardroom. The sight was bad. There was one doctor and a few
assistants tending to dozens of patients.

Sochor watched with guilt as men helplessly bled or suffered.
Then suddenly came a terrible noise: metal on metal grinding. Sochor returned to the hatch from where he had pulled the man. The
sound grew louder, echoing through the open hatch above the after fire room. Without notice a man gave Sochor a bucket of oil
and a fresh battle lantern, then told him to travel down to lubri-
cate the drive shaft, which was at risk of getting stuck. It was the
only drive shaft left. It was possible that the *Johnston* was losing her
last engine.

The engagement with the Japanese destroyers was kept up until they were four miles away. The first two destroyers had already
turned away, and Evans could make out the details of his third
opponent's superstructure through his binoculars. The carnage
was plain to see. Though his ship was outmatched in tonnage and
firepower, Evans was stronger willed than the Japanese destroyer
captains. The Japanese had the speed to outrun the *Johnston* and

gain the western edge of Taffy 3, completing their encirclement, but the *Johnston* was determined and the rest of the Japanese destroyers eventually followed the first two in retreat. Turning east, they waited until they were well out of effective range before launching their torpedo attack. The five healthy carriers were safe and Evans felt like the skipper of a battleship.

Men on the bridge recalled watching Evans during this time; amid all the smoke, blood, and cannon fire, he was beaming with pride. He was "so elated he could hardly talk. He strutted across his bridge and chortled, 'Now I've seen everything!'" reported Bob Hagen.

Though the *Johnston* had turned away seven Japanese destroyers, the celebration was short-lived. By 0842 the *Johnston* had closed to one mile of the *Gambier Bay*. She had capsized after listing heavily to port. Within two minutes this carrier would slip beneath the surface and take hundreds of her crew. Evans could not stop to rescue them. The other five carriers needed his smoke screen if they were to escape the Japanese cruisers that were in pursuit six miles to their northeast.

After the skirmish with the destroyers, Evans brought his ship southwest and continued to lay a smoke screen that would benefit from the west-moving wind. By now the aircraft of Taffy 2 were introducing their five-hundred-pounds bombs into the mix. At 0853 the heavy cruiser *Chikuma* was struck by a torpedo from a squadron of bombers. The Japanese were nursing four wounded cruisers, but the *Tone* and *Haguro* kept up pursuit at full speed.

By 0900 the *Yamato* and *Nagato* had come back south to within ten miles of the carriers. The Japanese battleships had actually made it south of the *Johnston*. At half speed Evans did not have the steam to outrun the Japanese.

By 0900 the *Johnston* was surrounded. The destroyer column she had just turned away was now in line behind the *Yamato* and *Nagato*, which were four miles to port. The cruisers *Tone* and *Haguro* were seven miles south. Five miles northwest of the *Johnston*, there was also a different column of four destroyers that was still attempting to close on the carriers' west flank. The *Johnston* fought these destroyers while to the south the remaining four destroyer escorts interposed themselves between the carriers and the *Haguro* and *Tone*.

At 0900 gun 54 stopped shooting. Unaware of the reason why, Evans sent Welch to investigate. "I worked my way aft, climbing over piles of dead sailors and wreckage. The gun resumed firing and I returned to the bridge, finding it deserted." Welch, realizing that Evans had likely left to command from the fantail, made his way aft.

There was nowhere for the *Johnston* to run except for southwest. The Japanese were faster and their guns had the range. At 0900 a six-inch shell from the *Yamato*'s secondary battery obliterated the starboard 40mm AA gun just forward of the bridge. Clouds of smoke rose up, obscuring Evans's view. Through shattered portholes black smoke poured, stinging Evans's eyes.

Additional hits tore the jury-rigged lines of communications connecting the bridge to the aft-steering compartment. Course changes were now being sent to the rudder by messenger on foot. "Sometimes a new change was sent before a prior one was executed," DiGardi recalled. This prompted Evans to abandon the bridge at 0920 because he had better command of the ship from the fantail.

Once Sochor returned from the dark smoke again, after having lubricated the last remaining drive shaft, he began to head for the manual steering room. But as he moved, a shell exploded behind him. The blast knocked him unconscious. When he woke up, blood and bodies surrounded him. Nobody around him was alive.

Departing from the bridge, Evans worked his way along the starboard edge of the ship, pushing aside piles of his dead as he went. The guns never stopped firing over his head. As he went, he stole glimpses of the destroyer column off to their right. Four miles away and moving southwest, the column was making its own attempt to close on the carriers. The other destroyer column closed on the carriers from farther east and was directly left of the *Johnston*, which was retreating south.

As Evans ran he gave steering orders. The movement of the ship made men all about him stumble. Each turn to starboard was made more difficult by the water pouring into the exposed parts of the ship. "With two or three men trying to turn the rudder we could barely make it move," recalled Rogers, a sailor from a useless ammunition room who had gone to move the rudders after running out of shells.

Other men were running to find Evans and receive further turning orders. As Evans went, he passed dozens of sailors who were gathered underneath the shelter of the starboard 40mm gun director amidships, just even with the second stack. Evans saw them but did not stop to order them to join him on the fantail. He had just moved on when, behind him, a shell exploded in that exact space beneath the 40mm director. Evans looked up behind him just as dozens of limbs fell into the sea.

Evans was completely vulnerable, though among his sailors he led bravely. Once he reached the fantail, he continued to give steering orders, shouting directly down through the hatch in the fantail that opened into the aft steering compartment. On her stern *Johnston* was fitted with two depth charge racks, two depth charge launchers, and two antiaircraft positions that Evans had to work around as he moved between the aft steering hatch and the ship's rails while tracking the fight.

From 0922 onward Evans shouted orders down to the men controlling the rudder. Nearly a hundred men crowded there, looking for a job. Evans had orders for all of them. He sent men forward to find wounded. Other men were sent to unhook the floater nets and life rafts.

Evans was shirtless and bloodied; the remaining shreds of his shirt were quickly burned off by the muzzle blast of the after five-inch gun, 55, as it continued to fire at Japanese destroyers to the rear. The battleships were an afterthought when compared to the hornetlike destroyers stinging the *Johnston* at will. At four miles the Japanese destroyers began to circle the *Johnston*.

Taffy 2 aircraft now began harassing the remaining two heavy cruisers, and the carriers of Taffy 3 looked like they might escape. The *Johnston*, however, was in the middle of a terrible fight.

Bob Hagen and his team remained in the gun director after the bridge had been abandoned. "The place was full of smoke; our eyes were streaming and we were coughing and choking as we carried out our duties. There were two cruisers on our port [*Chokai* and *Chikuma*]; another two cruisers ahead of us [the *Haguro* and

Tone] and several destroyers on our starboard side. We desperately traded shots first with one group and then the other," Hagen later wrote.

On the fantail Evans watched as aircraft from Taffy 2 formed in the sky for their attack, coming into and out of the smoke with ease. They had plenty of targets, and attacked as the *Johnston* continued southwest. This was the only direction that she could travel without steering directly into an enemy column.

The *Johnston* continued to receive shell hits in the forward part of the ship. Several sailors on the bow recalled that destroyers were firing from such close range that shells passed directly through the ship and never exploded. Clean holes were made through the chief petty officers' wardroom, forward of the bridge and one level belowdecks.

Every hit was felt. Evans's instinct told him that the end was near. He handed off command of the rudder to Clyde Burnett and ran from the fantail toward his personal gig, which was strapped to the starboard side, just below the bridge. In it he would load as many wounded men as possible before casting it off. As he ran forward along the starboard side, he passed over fresh corpses. The loss of life certainly insulted Evans, who had a deep reverence for his men's lives.

As Evans ran, he looked across the ship. While passing the space between the after torpedo rack and gun 53, Evans saw Lieutenant Welch running down the port side of the ship toward the fantail. Welch had left the bridge earlier on orders to learn why gun 54 had stopped firing. Welch was returning to the fantail after finding the bridge abandoned. Evans made eye contact with Welch and carried on.

On the starboard side, Evans reached his private gig and worked alongside several men to untie it. Quickly Evans got the craft alongside the ship, and ordered two men to assist him with bringing wounded aboard. Evans then ran back to the fantail. As he did, shells landed yards off, sending water cascading over the deck. This evaporated instantly because of the heat of the fires below. The soles of boots were melting and it was clear that the fires alone could claim the ship.

On Evans's way back aft, an explosion behind him caused a chill to run down his spine. A shell violently crashed into the gun director through its port side, cracking its casing and exiting out the back before tumbling through the air and into the ocean. Unsure whether or not his gunnery officer had survived, Evans continued toward the fantail.

In the director, there were too many targets for Bob Hagen to count. Though the smoke from the destruction of gun 52 was clouding his vision, he could see targets—they were that close. Then a shell hit the starboard 40mm gun ahead of the bridge and Hagen could not see a thing. The black smoke blowing into his face thickened, forcing Hagen to abandon the director by 0925.

Back on the fantail, Evans found Clyde Burnett still in command of steering. Many men were there. Welch was there instinctively setting the depth charges to safe. Evans had taught his men to do this in case of a sinking. There were two large racks on the stern and three smaller ones on each side of gun 54. As Evans ran to help disarm these, the concussion of gun 55 reverberated through his body. His shirt had been burned off, and his skin was burned. His muscles ached from steadying himself on the swerving ship for over two hours.

Gun 55 continued to fight until 0929. Then a direct hit landed. With this, gun 54 became the only gun to remain shooting. Bob Hollenbaugh was fighting with this gun until the very end. On the fantail Evans led, from the very spot where he had taken command of the ship twelve months before.

At 0930 the Japanese landed a shot that took out the last engine. Evans felt the ship lurch forward and drift. Without a moment's hesitation, he began to prepare to abandon ship.

With the *Johnston* dead in the water, two Japanese destroyers closed to within a thousand yards and circled like predators. "They were shooting at us like a bunch of Indians attacking a prairie schooner," Hagen recalled. Slowly the *Johnston* rolled to a stop before coming to rest twenty thousand yards northeast of the Taffy 3 carriers. Five of the carriers were safe and moving west, with the *Dennis*, *John C. Butler*, *Raymond*, and *Heermann* trailing behind and still laying smoke. The *Hoel*, *Samuel B. Roberts*, and *Gambier Bay* had been sunk.

Evans could hear down belowdecks the loaders of gun 54 tearing their throats, demanding "more shells," while the rest of the crew gathered for their swim or were already in the water. The railing of the *Johnston* looked like the front step to a shoe shop. Beneath the taffrail dozens of pairs of shoes were neatly set; the sailors, obliging Navy regulations, had removed their shoes before jumping into the water. At 0945 Evans gave the saddest order a captain can give. "Abandon ship."

Evans found Clyde Burnett and confirmed with him that the depth charges were safe. Then, with three other sailors, Burnett rolled the charges off the ship. Evans left these men to this task and began running toward the bow, bellowing his order to abandon ship. Evans would be the last off, it was certain.

As he ran forward, Evans was shouting at the tops of his lungs, repeating his order. Adrenaline fueled him as he moved. Several other officers went up the other side of the ship, repeating the order to anybody they found alive. In the last moments of the battle, Lieutenant Welch ran along one side of the ship, parallel to Evans, shouting, "Abandon ship."

Most men did not hesitate to jump in, but many had not swum since boot camp in Michigan's Great Lakes. Quickly nets were thrown overboard and men began to cling to them. Those with life jackets also became couples in the water.

Evans spotted Lieutenant DiGardi before he jumped off and ordered him to destroy all classified material. Then Evans continued on up the ship toward the bow. "Abandon ship." The cries went out from Evans, and still Hollenbaugh's gun 54 fought. The *Johnston* was dead in the water and listing nearly twenty degrees to port when Bob Hollenbaugh relayed the order for the men in gun 54 to give up the fight.

As Evans ran he saw that some men were already in the water. Nearing the bridge Evans noticed wounded being carried from the officers' wardroom into rafts alongside the ship. Evans passed Edward Block, glad to see him alive. Lieutenant Welch was inflating Block's life vest; he had stopped Block before the barber crawled over the *Johnston*'s rail and landed in the water without his vest inflated. Block was concussed and on two shots of morphine following the hits taken to the bridge. He would have drowned had it not been for Lieutenant Welch stopping him and inflating his jacket.

While the sailors were gathering to enter the sea, a Japanese destroyer closed to four hundred yards and began sending shells into the *Johnston*. The rounds passed directly through and shook the ship so violently that some men could not stay on their feet. Men fell into the ocean rather than jumping, some hitting their heads and drowning immediately. By 0955 there were dozens of sailors grouped together a hundred yards from the ship and swimming away. They knew to swim away from the *Johnston* or they'd risk getting pulled under by the suction as she sank.

Evans reached the bow shortly before 1000. Evans passed a sailor he might have recognized as Bob Sochor. Sochor appeared black because of his efforts to save men in the after fire room; he leaned against the rail, preparing to jump in. Sochor later recalled the moment when Evans passed by with a thousand-yard stare as he went looking for wounded men to help into the water.

Once he reached the bow, Evans began traveling aft down the other side of the *Johnston*. Evans was trying hard to keep himself moving as the Japanese destroyers continued to put shells through his ship. The starboard side was not safe to use to exit into the sea because the destroyers were so close. Some Japanese sailors fired small arms at the *Johnston*.

Evans traveled to the port side of the ship and helped wounded get into life vests and climb into rafts already in the water. All that was required was to step forward into the water, which was about level with the *Johnston*'s port-side main deck because of her list. By 1002 there were nearly a hundred men in the water. Men on rafts, nets, or debris were very quickly about a quarter mile away from the *Johnston*.

DiGardi recalled that he "went out of the deck house to the

main deck and saw Jack Bechdel at the rail trying to get over. His stump was dressed but he was too weak to get over, I took him by the back of the neck and seat of his pants and gave him an assist. Almost immediately, there was a direct hit behind me and the next thing I knew, I was blown out of my shoes and socks and was 30 feet from the ship and in the water."

From the port side, Evans could see his captain's gig filled with dozens of men, though it was in danger of foundering because of holes from shrapnel. In the water, men watched as the hulk of the former world-beating *Johnston* was pummeled.

Hagen saw Evans helping men over the edge until the end. Moments before the ship went down, Evans stood on the bow and saluted his crew in the water beyond him. Then Evans disappeared as he ran aft to help more men. Some say they saw Evans at the end climbing into a raft.

In the water there were two floater net groups forming, and within minutes, they had drifted a quarter of a mile from *Johnston*. Some men were in the water, lying on their backs, aware of the rumor that a depth charge would not hurt if you were on your back. "Not true," Ed Block recalled. Most men expected the charges to detonate, not trusting that they had been set on safe. One did explode, and the pressure sent a shock wave through everybody in the water, though nobody's bowels erupted.

The sailors of the *Johnston* were in the water for fifty-four hours. Those who claimed that Evans was in the water also said that blood loss, exposure, or shark attack claimed his life during the first twenty-four hours. He also could have gone down with his ship.

Lieutenant Welch recalled becoming very emotional: "Seeing

my home go down, I felt my eyes welling with tears. But, I thought, Welch, you might need the liquid, so I ceased this un-seamanly display of emotion." The *Johnston* went down by the stern, her bow rising high into the air, her anchor swinging until she disappeared.

All the men did not initially form together in the water, wary of Japanese ship captains who might fire on a large group. After the *Johnston* sank, one destroyer steered very close by, and a portion of the crew lined the rail. Many of Evans's sailors dove into the sea thinking that they were going to be shot at. Some men thought the Japanese would throw grenades.

Most *Johnston* officers had thrown away their .45 service pistols before entering the water. The sight of the Japanese sailors looking down at them from the destroyer *Yukikaze* was powerful. "It appeared to me that every man on her deck was standing at attention, like a muster, giving us one big salute. Her gold tasseled flag with the rising sun was hoisted to her mast sharply." This Jap destroyer was going slow enough to produce no bow wake, leaving the waters relatively still as it passed. Then one of the Japanese destroyer men tossed something to one of the American destroyer men.

Many sailors went ducking below the waves, escaping the shrapnel they expected to come from a grenade blast. "It was a No. 2½ can of tomatoes, packed somewhere in Arkansas, U.S.A. Three years of war and they were still eating USA canned tomatoes," recalled Clint Carter. Similar to boxers acknowledging each other after a fight, the Japanese had acknowledged their American foe with a salute and a parting gift.

With one battle ended, another ordeal came. After two days in the water, many men hallucinated, seized by the idea they could swim underwater, enter the ship, and find food, water, or a cup of coffee in the galley. Some hallucinated about a case of beer they had stashed in their locker, and swam to their death to go and find it. It took a night to learn that those men at risk of hallucinating needed to be tied down. The first night unsupervised men went out to attempt to find the *Johnston* or swim for shore. Their splashes would wake up the men, but often too late for others to pull them back before they were eaten by sharks.

The survivors would not get picked up for fifty-four hours. In his *Saturday Evening Post* article, Hagen wrote that "while I was clinging to a floater net and puffing on an imaginary cigarette through swollen lips, I thought about that conversation with the skipper. I thought about the stupendous pre-commissioning party we'd pitched in Seattle, and about the ice cream and cake the skipper had promised us for our first birthday at sea."

Of the USS *Johnston*'s 327 officers and crew, 141 were eventually rescued by American ships. Many more than that had gone into the water, but an unknown number drowned, or died of exposure, or fell victim to sharks. Ernest Evans's exact fate remains unknown.

At one point the ponderous IJN *Yamato* herself glided by the survivors of one of the American ships, and this time Japanese sailors did start to shoot at them with small arms, but a sour-looking officer quickly appeared on the bridge wing high up; he bellowed and gesticulated at his men to stop. It was Admiral Takeo Kurita. He wanted no more bloodshed. Instead, he issued orders for his remaining vessels to rejoin with him, and they retreated. Ugaki was mortified. "Why?" He pointed south. "The enemy is that way." A cheer went up from the men when the story circulated that they had turned north to engage Halsey.

At a time when it appeared that he was in a position to press his attack home, Kurita sailed away, and that has remained the central question about the Battle off Samar: why?

From Kurita's standpoint, the Japanese had long proven the critical importance of air superiority, and he had been sent into battle with no air cover whatsoever. Had he pressed his attack, his ships would have been obliterated by the combination of land-based aircraft and those of Halsey's fleet carriers, which were surely returning at flank speed. He had already lost one of his two super battleships; he had begun the day with six heavy cruisers, now he had two. *Kumano* limped away after her bow was blown off, and during the fight *Suzuya*, *Chokai*, and *Chikuma* were all sunk by the combination of surface and air attacks. There was nothing to accomplish at Leyte, and he agreed with his late commander, Admiral Yamamoto, that vainglorious sacrifices were foolish. And above all else Kurita, an experienced destroyer captain, would have found it inconceivable that Operation Sho-Go had been wrecked by one division of American destroyers and destroyer escorts fighting so savagely, so far above their capabilities and with such indomitable will. At one point he saw one of his cruisers ablaze and believed that he must be facing a superior cruiser force; in reality, the *Johnston* had run out of armor-piercing shells and was firing star shells, and it was the white-hot phosphorous that had ignited the fires.

After his withdrawal from the Philippines, Kurita was relieved of command, and to insulate him from assassination attempts, he was removed to Etajima Island in Hiroshima Bay and named the commandant of the Imperial Naval College. Through a long retirement, he remained controversial: reviled by many for not sacrificing himself, his ships, and his men in glory for the emperor, and respected by others for saving the lives of the tens of thousands of seamen under his command. After the war he was reduced to finding work as a scrivener and a masseur. He tended his garden, he drank, and true to his habit of decades, he offered no excuses. Only once did he say that his turning away was a mistake induced by fatigue. Near the close of his life, he told an old schoolmate, probably with the truth of a dying declaration, that he broke off the action because it was not worth the waste of any more men. He died at eighty-eight on December 19, 1977.

Admiral Ugaki, however, was granted his wish to die for the emperor when he was made the commander of the remaining kamikaze pilots. Almost simultaneously with Japan's surrender, Ugaki led a final squadron of eleven planes, and they sacrificed themselves while causing no appreciable damage.

The legacy of Ernest Evans is entirely different. Clyde Burnett gave his opinion of the *Johnston*'s skipper some forty years later. He wrote in a diary, "If the Captain hadn't made the torpedo run as he did on that 25th day of October, 1944, we would have lost six carriers instead of one and it is entirely possible that we could have lost the beachhead on Leyte Island as well."

Evans earned a Bronze Star and a Navy Cross for his actions, upgraded in September 1945 to the Congressional Medal of Honor. The decorations were presented to his wife, who continued to raise their two sons in Long Beach, California. The boys, Ernest Jr. and David, were thirteen and twelve, respectively, at the time of the battle. The citation read as follows:

For conspicuous gallantry and intrepidity at the risk of his life above and beyond the call of duty as Commanding Officer of the USS

Johnston, in action against major units of the enemy Japanese Fleet during the Battle off Samar on October 25, 1944. The first to lay a smoke screen and to open fire as an enemy task force vastly superior in number, firepower and armor rapidly approached, Commander Evans gallantly diverted the powerful blasts of hostile guns from the lightly armed and armored carriers under his protection, launching the first torpedo attack when the Johnston *came under straddling Japanese shellfire. Undaunted by damage sustained under the terrific volume of fire, he unhesitatingly joined others of his group to provide fire support during subsequent torpedo attacks against the Japanese and, outshooting and outmaneuvering the enemy as he consistently interposed his vessel between the hostile Fleet units and our carriers despite the crippling loss of engine power and communications with steering aft, shifted command to the fantail, shouted steering orders through an open hatch to men turning the rudder by hand and battled furiously until the* Johnston, *burning and shuddering from a mortal blow, lay dead in the water after three hours of fierce combat. Seriously wounded early in the engagement, Commander Evans, by his indomitable courage and brilliant professional skill, aided materially in turning back the enemy during a critical phase of the action. His valiant fighting spirit throughout this historic battle will endure as an inspiration to all who served with him.*

USS *Johnston* impacted the seabed stern first at around 1015 on the morning of October 25, 1944, two days less than a year after her commissioning in the Seattle–Tacoma shipyard. Her remains were discovered in October 2019 more than twenty thousand feet beneath the surface, the deepest WWII wreck discovered up to that time. The debris field was visited and the identification made in the spring of 2021 by a remote vehicle from the research vessel *Petrel*. This expedition brought back images of the ship, which had lain unseen for seventy-seven years. Upon hitting the bottom, the rear part of the vessel had broken apart, but her forward two-thirds remained impressively intact. The bow sits upright, her identifying 557 clearly discernible. Just as they were when the ship went down, the forward two five-inch guns are still trained to starboard, engaging Japanese warships to the last.

Note on Sources

Ernest Evans is likely the last naval hero of World War II to have lacked a book-length biography until now, and the author expresses his gratitude to the United States Naval History and Heritage Command for making available the hundreds of pages in Evans's service record.

The finest traditional treatment of the Battle off Samar is James D. Hornfischer, *Last Stand of the Tin Can Sailors: The Extraordinary World War II Story of the U.S. Navy's Finest Hour* (Bantam, 2004), and a highly original perspective is Evan Thomas's quadruple biography of Admiral Halsey, Commander Evans, Admiral Kurita, and Admiral Ugaki in *Sea of Thunder: Four Commanders and the Last Great Naval Campaign 1941–1945* (Simon & Schuster, 2006). Thomas also wrote an insightful analysis of Admiral Takeo Kurita and his decision to break away from the action off Samar in "Understanding Kurita's Mysterious Retreat" in *Naval History Magazine* vol. 18, no. 5 (October 2004).

An authentic view of Evans as a commander was left by his gunnery officer in Robert C. Hagen, "We Asked for the Jap Fleet—and
Got It," in the *Saturday Evening Post* of May 26, 1945, now archived
(behind a subscription paywall) at https://www.saturdayevening
post.com/subscribe-to-issue/?issue=19450526.

Available online via the Naval History and Heritage Command
is a fine service chronology of the USS *Johnston* by Robert J. Cress-
man, "*Johnston* I (DD-557) 1943–1944," at https://www.history.navy
.mil/research/histories/ship-histories/danfs/j/johnston-i.html. The
Navy also commemorates Evans's career at https://www.history
.navy.mil/content/history/nhhc/research/library/research-guides
/modern-biographical-files-ndl/modern-bios-e/evans-ernest-edwin
.html.

The U.S. Naval Academy honors Evans's gallantry with a selection of brief pieces at https://usnamemorialhall.org/index.php/ER
NEST_E._EVANS,_CDR,_USN.

A good source for the desperate struggles of ships caught behind
the Japanese line of conquest after Pearl Harbor is L. Klemen, https://
warfare.gq/dutcheastindies/war_sea.html.

For good information on the *Fletcher*-class destroyers and their
capabilities, see Alan Raven, *Fletcher-Class Destroyers: Anatomy of the
Ship* (Naval Institute Press, 1986).

Secondary sources on the general Battle of Leyte Gulf include
Thomas J. Cutler, *The Battle of Leyte Gulf, 23–26 October 1944* (Naval
Institute Press, 2001); James A. Field, *The Japanese at Leyte Gulf: The Sho
Operation* (Princeton University Press, 1947); William F. Halsey, *The
Battle for Leyte Gulf* (Naval Institute Press, 1983); Samuel Eliot Morison,
Leyte: June 1944–January 1945, which is volume 12 of *History of United*

States Naval Operations in World War II (Castle Books, 2001, reprint); David Sears, *The Last Epic Naval Battle: Voices from Leyte Gulf* (Praeger Publishers, 2005); H. P. Willmott, *The Battle of Leyte Gulf: The Last Fleet Action* (Indiana University Press, 2005); and C. Vann Woodward, *The Battle for Leyte Gulf* (Battery Press, 1989).

Acknowledgments

This book is published with great pride. It represents what is accomplished when generous scholars and professionals prescribe their abilities to a single vision. It also represents an addition to the legacy of Captain Ernest Edwin Evans and his crew who fought and died for our freedom.

I owe a particular debt of thanks and gratitude to my late father, James D. Hornfischer, for encouraging me as a first-time author. Dad is known as an amazingly accomplished historian and bestselling author but was also a passionate supporter of his family and each of our personal interests. As I look back, I see many of our family trips as stepping-stones toward my personal and professional development.

I give credit to my father for nurturing a care for history in me, from Scouts overnights onboard the USS *Lexington* in Corpus Christi, Texas, to visits of the USS *Midway* at San Diego and USS *Massachusetts* in Fall River, Massachusetts. If there were World War

II ships, museums, or air shows anywhere near our family travels, side excursions to these destinations were added to our itinerary.

Additionally, my love and respect of history was piqued early on as our family attended many World War II ship reunions where Dad was often the keynote speaker, and we were introduced to the stories and many heroes. Through these trips I was fortunate enough to meet many veterans of Taffy 3, and the impressions their honor and sacrifice made on me will last my lifetime.

I thank Commander Evans's granddaughter Deborah Evans Mott for kindly offering her knowledge of her grandfather's nature. Her father (Commander Evans's son, Ernest Evans Jr.) was a Marine colonel. He followed in his father's footsteps and carried himself with great dignity in his life. These shared family accounts helped bring his personality to life throughout this book.

I would like to thank others for invaluable resources, the ones that gave this book its rich historic depth. Thanks to Tristen Healy and members of the crew of the USS *Cassin Young* Museum in Charlestown, Massachusetts, I was able to receive an impression of the scope of authority that Commander Evans wielded from the bridge. Thanks to material from Malvina Bardoni from the Naval History and Heritage Command, I was able to trace Commander Evans's career through the 1930s up to his assignment to the USS *Johnston*. Thanks to Mathew Crosby at the National Archive in Saint Louis, Chris McDougal with the National Museum of the Pacific War, and Kim McKeithan with the National Archive in Washington, DC, I was able to cover missing periods in Commander Evans's early career and provide real substance regarding his family's life while he was in service. Thanks to Joe Crittenden and Barbara Foreman with the Cherokee Nation Educational

Services and to Gano Perez with the Creek Nations Historic and Cultural Preservations Department, I was able to understand the breadth of influence that the Evans family had in eastern Oklahoma.

Recently on the public stage, I recognized deep-ocean explorers Victor Vescovo and Parks Stephenson for their identification and survey of the wreck of the USS *Johnston* nearly seventy-seven years after its last voyage. The analysis of the wreckage that their mission garnered provided new insights about the choreography of the Battle of Leyte Gulf that I used to illustrate the destroyer's final hour.

I am grateful to my Dutton/Penguin Random House publishing team. I would like to thank John Parsley for his leadership, and my editor, Charlotte Peters, for bringing this project into the endzone. She was professional and approachable for a first-time author to work with. I appreciate her taking this inherited project and treating it with such high regard and respect. I would also like to thank my original editor, Brent Howard, for the careful attention he gave to this book and for the insights he offered me during the early phases of the writing process. He understood the vision Dad and I had and the importance of Captain Evans's heroic story reaching a wider audience.

I would like to thank the knowledgeable and prolific writer Mr. James Haley. He gave of his valuable time and expert editorial assistance with framework and structure to help me craft chapters and navigate the complex battleline narrative. He was a source of guidance that I drew from often. I am grateful for his friendship. I would like to thank John Bruning and John Wukovits for their editorial comments when I needed the support here and there throughout the writing process. Their professional tenor gave me direction when needed.

And last and foremost of all, thanks to my family: my mother, Sharon Hornfischer; my siblings, Grace and Hutch; and my grandfather Dave R. Hornfischer for their unwavering and many-faceted support of me and one another through the journey of loss, love, and acceptance we have been traveling since my father's passing.

About the Authors

James D. Hornfischer was a writer, literary agent, and book editor. He was the author of the *New York Times* bestsellers *Neptune's Inferno*, *The Last Stand of the Tin Can Sailors*, *Ship of Ghosts*, and *The Fleet at Flood Tide*, all widely acclaimed accounts of the U.S. Navy in the Pacific during World War II, as well as the upcoming *Who Can Hold the Sea*. His books have received numerous awards, including the Samuel Eliot Morison Award for Naval Literature and the Naval Historical Foundation Distinguished Service Award. James D. Hornfischer died in 2021.

David James Hornfischer is a graduate of the University of Arkansas with a bachelor's degree from the Walton School of Business. David has had a lifelong interest in history, particularly World War II history, where he had a front-row seat throughout his father's military historian career. Since the age of six, David has been his father's office assistant and book box carrier. David was fond of book signings, where he could be of extra help with setting up books. Through the years, as David's acumen and interest grew, he became an invaluable research assistant for various history projects. *Destroyer Captain: The Life of Ernest E. Evans* is his first book.

Today, David is leaning into his interest of history and is pursuing a career as a history teacher. David lives in Austin, Texas.